TIME AND MONEY

Using Time-Value Analysis in Financial Planning

Eighth Edition

Robert M. Crowe, Ph.D.
CLU, ChFC, CPCU, CFP

Distributed by
Keir Educational Resources
Jack C. Keir, Inc.
4785 Emerald Way
Middletown, OH 45044
1-800-795-5347
E-mail: customerservice@keirsuccess.com
www.keirsuccess.com

All efforts have been made to ensure the accuracy of the contents of this material. However, should any errors be detected, Keir Educational Resources would greatly appreciate being informed of them.

Information in this material is subject to change without notice. No part of this material may be reproduced or transmitted in any form or by any means or for any purpose without the express written permission of Keir Educational Resources.

FOREWORD

A great many of the financial transactions in which people routinely engage involve paying or receiving money early and receiving or paying back money later. For example, financing the purchase of a home entails receiving money now and paying money back later. Buying mutual fund shares entails paying out money now and receiving back money later. The same types of trade-offs between money now and money later are made when we buy life insurance, put money in a bank savings account, establish a trust, invest in real estate, borrow from a credit union, decide to lease rather than buy a car, or engage in many other types of financial transactions.

As will be explained in this book, however, money now and money later are not of equal value. A tool is needed to analyze the difference in the two values. That analytical tool is the time value of money. One of the leading financial educators in the U.S. has written that "... of all the techniques used in finance, none is more important that the concept of time value of money, or discounted cash flow (DCF) analysis."[1]p. 196. This book is designed to help you use time value of money as a tool for more intelligent financial decision making.

I owe a great deal of gratitude to many people who have helped me to create this book. Thousands of students have read it over the years and helped me weed out errors and more clearly explain certain concepts. Several former colleagues of mine at The American College have reviewed early drafts of the manuscript and helped me reduce the fuzziness of some of my thought processes. And many typists and editors, especially my wife, Pat, have struggled with my handwriting and with the complex layout of some of the formulas in the text. To all of these good people, my sincere thanks.

Robert M. Crowe
Cordova, Tennessee
February, 2002

---

[1] Eugene F. Brigham, *Fundamentals of Financial Management*, 7th ed. (Orlando, FL: The Dryden Press), p. 196.

TO

PAT

with whom, during the past 42+ years,
I've spent a lot of time and money

TABLE OF CONTENTS

CHAPTER ONE - TIME VALUE OF MONEY: BASIC CONCEPTS AND APPLICATIONS

TABLE OF CONTENTS (CONT'D)

TABLE OF CONTENTS (CONT'D)

Losing Patience with Your Financial Calculator

Are you using the Hewlett-Packard® HP12C Calculator?

Keir Educational Resources conducts online calculator classes to help you learn the keystrokes necessary to help you evaluate time value of money as a tool for more intelligent financial decision-making.

This class is conveniently scheduled for just two hours a day for two days from 11 a.m. to 1 p.m. Eastern time. **The cost is $75.** You can attend the class from your office or your home! All you need is a phone line to join the class on a conference call and an internet connection to view the PowerPoint presentation. Call **800-795-5347** or visit our website at www.keirsuccess.com to find a complete schedule.

Here is what students are saying about this great class:

"This first class was absolutely fabulous. I would highly recommend it to everyone. I know tomorrow will be more difficult but I am looking forward to it. I am actually excited about a calculator! Great teacher! Great, simple method." ~ *Anne*

"I thought the program was awesome. The explanation of why you used certain buttons was a great help. I was never taught that way, it was always just memorize the keys. Even as a lender, I was taught what buttons to push, not why." ~ *Paul*

"I thought this was the best educational experience for the money I have had. I would like to see more advanced calculator classes. That calculator can do so much and is so complex, I have been using mine for 10 years and I bet I don't know ½ of what it can do." ~ *Noelle*

Contact us today!

800-795-5347

www.keirsuccess.com

Chapter One

Time Value of Money: Basic Concepts and Applications

THE BASICS OF TIME VALUE

1.   Why is it that when individuals take out a loan they must repay more money than they borrowed? Why is it that a supplier of materials you use in your business offers you a discount from the full amount of the invoice if you pay within 30 days? Why does a savings and loan association credit depositors' savings accounts with interest? Why is it that when you deposit a perfectly good check in your checking account, the bank may deny you access to the money for a few days? Why is it inadequate for an investor to evaluate a proposed investment project on the basis of its payback period, that is, the number of years it will take for the total cash inflows from the project to equal the initial cash outlay? Why does the winner of a lottery prize of $1 million after taxes, payable in $100,000 annual installments over ten years, actually receive less than $1 million of value?

2.   The answers to all of these and dozens of similar questions center on the time value of money. These questions arise in all fields of business and personal financial planning, real estate, marketing, investments, accounting, insurance, banking, and many other fields.

3.   Some erroneously believe that a dollar is a dollar is a dollar. The fact is that dollars to be paid or received in different time periods have different values. Ask yourself these questions. When would you rather receive your federal income tax refund check – as soon as you file your return or three months later? When would you rather collect the rent from the tenants in your apartment building – at the beginning of each month or at the end?

Opportunity Cost

4.   Solely on the basis of intuition, most people probably would conclude, quite properly, that they would prefer to receive

the money sooner rather than later. Why? Because the sooner they receive the money, the sooner they can use it, either spend it or invest it, for their own benefit. If they wait for the money, they incur what economists call an "opportunity cost." The opportunity cost of an activity (in this case, waiting to receive the money) is the value of the lost opportunity to engage in the best alternative activity (in this case, spending or investing the money now) with the same resource (in this case, the specified sum of money).

5.   Conversely, again strictly on the basis of intuition, most would properly conclude that if they must pay out a specified sum of money, they would prefer to pay it later rather than sooner. Why? Because the longer they can delay the payment, the longer they can use the money, either spend it or invest it, for their own benefit. If they pay the money early, they incur an opportunity cost.

The Role of Interest

6.   Since a given sum of money due in different time periods does not have the same value, a tool is needed in order to make the different values comparable. That tool is interest, which can be viewed as a way of quantifying the opportunity cost incurred by one who waits to receive money or who gives up the opportunity to delay paying it.

7.   For example, if you deposit $1,000 in a savings account and leave it there for one year, you expect to have more than $1,000 in the account at the end of that time. You expect your account to earn interest. You postponed the use of your money and, instead, allowed the bank to use it. You incurred an opportunity cost. The interest the bank gives you is compensation to you for having done so.

8.   To reverse the situation, assume that a loan you took out at your bank will mature in one year, at which time you are obligated to pay $10,000. If you repay the loan today, one year early, you believe you should be required to pay less than the full $10,000. If you forgo the opportunity to delay the repayment, you should be compensated in return by having the amount payable reduced.

9.   The specific interest rate that should be used to quantify opportunity cost is made up of two components: a risk-free rate and a risk premium. At a minimum, the opportunity cost of letting someone else use your money is the rate of return you could have earned by investing it in a perfectly safe instrument. A reasonable measure of this minimum opportunity cost is the rate of interest available on three-month U.S. Treasury bills. These bills are always available and, for all practical purposes, are risk-free. At the time of this writing, three-month T-bills were yielding an unusually low rate of about 2 percent on an annual basis.

10.   In addition, most situations in which you allow someone else to use your money entail some risk of loss for you. For example, the market value of your investment instrument may decline because of rising interest rates. The purchasing power of your principal sum may be eroded by inflation. The person or organization using your funds may default on scheduled interest and principal payments. Tax laws may be changed to lower the aftertax return on your investment. These and other types of risk associated with letting someone else use your funds should be reflected in a risk premium, or add-on to the risk-free opportunity cost of money. The higher the degree of risk, the greater should be the risk premium and, therefore, the higher should be the interest rate you require.

Simple Interest versus Compound Interest

11.   There are two ways of computing interest. *Simple interest* is computed by applying an interest rate to only an original principal sum. *Compound interest* is computed by applying an interest rate to the total of an original principal sum and all interest credited to it in earlier time periods.

12.   To illustrate the difference, assume $100 is deposited in an account that earns 6 percent simple interest per year. At the end of each year, the account will be credited with $6.00 of interest. At the end of five years, there will be $130 in the account (if no withdrawals have been made), as shown on the left-hand side of table 1.1.

TABLE 1.1
Accumulation of $100 in Five Years
at 6% Simple and Compound Interest per Year

	Simple Interest			Compound Interest		
Year	Principal Sum	Interest	Ending Balance	Principal Sum	Interest	Ending Balance
1	$100.00	$6.00	$106.00	$100.00	$6.00	$106.00
2	$100.00	$6.00	$112.00	$106.00	$6.36	$112.36
3	$100.00	$6.00	$118.00	$112.36	$6.74	$119.10
4	$100.00	$6.00	$124.00	$119.10	$7.15	$126.25
5	$100.00	$6.00	$130.00	$126.25	$7.58	$133.82

13.   If, instead, the account earns 6 percent compound interest per year, it will grow to a larger amount, again as shown in table 1.1. The extra $3.82 in the account when it is credited with compound interest is interest earned on previous interest earnings.

14.   Notice the difference in the annual amount by which the account grows when compound rather than simple interest is credited. The balance grows by a constant amount, $6.00 per year, when simple interest is used. In the case of compound interest, however, the account balance grows by an increasing amount each year. The *rate* of growth, however, remains the same, 6 percent in this illustration.

15.   Most of the day-to-day situations calling for a recognition or calculation of the time value of money involve compound interest, rather than simple interest. Hence, the balance of this book will deal only with compound interest.

Compounding versus Discounting

16.   The process by which money today, a *present value*, grows over time to a larger amount, a *future value*, is called *compounding*. The process by which money due in the future, a *future value*, is reduced over time to a smaller amount today, a *present value*, is called *discounting*.

17.   Figure 1.1 shows the difference between present and future value, with compound interest as the link between the two. Compounding may be viewed as a movement up the curve, while discounting may be viewed as a movement down the curve. Note also that the link between present and future value in figure 1.1 is shown as a curve, rather than as a straight line, to reflect the application of compound interest rather than simple interest. When compound interest is used, the future value rises each year by an increasing amount of money (or the present value declines by a decreasing amount of money).

Figure 1.1
Compound Interest as the Link between Present Value and
Future Value

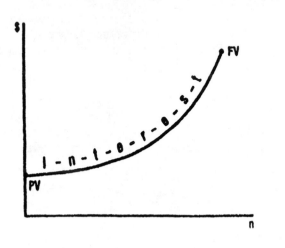

This figure depicts compound interest as the link between the
two values. Dollar amounts are reflected by the vertical axis,
and the number of periods during which compounding or
discounting occurs is reflected on the horizontal axis. As one
moves up the curve (compounding), the future value grows by
increasing amounts. As one moves down the curve (discounting),
the present value declines by decreasing amounts.

18.   Two major factors influence the shape of the curve in
figure 1.1. These are: (a) the number of periods over which
compounding or discounting occurs, and (b) the interest rate
used in the compounding or discounting process. All other
things being equal, the greater the number of periods, the greater
is the length of the curve. Consequently, as the number of
periods is increased, the difference between the present value
and the future value also increases. Similarly, all other things

being equal, the greater the interest rate, the steeper is the slope of the curve. Thus, as the interest rate is increased, the difference between the present value and the future value also increases.

19.   These relationships among the number of periods (n), the interest rate (i), the future value of money (FV), and the present value of money (PV) may be summarized as follows: in compounding, FV moves in the same direction as n and i (it increases as they increase); in discounting, PV moves in the opposite direction from n and i (it decreases as they increase).

20.   Note also that there are four key variables in the most basic problems involving the time value of money. They are the number of periods, the interest rate, the present value, and the future value. In these problems, you will be given three of the variables and be called upon to solve for the fourth. In more complex time-value problems, there are four or five variables, including the interest rate, the amount of each payment in a series of payments, the number of payments, the present value, and the future value. You will be given three or four of the variables and asked to compute the fourth or fifth. And, some apparently complex time-value problems are simply combinations of two or more of the basic four-variable problems that are linked together.[1]

The Power of Compound Interest

21.   Of course, your concern with compound interest is not so much with the shape of a curve as with the effect that compound interest has on the time value of money. That effect is extremely powerful, especially when a high interest rate or a long period of time is involved. For example, in the year 1980, the Consumer Price Index, a fairly good measure of the rate of inflation, rose by 13.5 percent over the preceding year. If that rate of inflation had continued throughout the decade of the 1980s and on up to the turn of the century, the same bag of groceries that cost $100 in 1980 would have cost about $355 in 1990! By 2002, it would have cost over $1,621!!

22.　One more example will help to emphasize the point. Peter Minuit is said to have purchased the island of Manhattan in the year 1626 for about $24 worth of beads. If instead of buying Manhattan at the beginning of 1626, he had put the $24 into a bank account paying 6 percent compound interest per year and left the money there continuously, at the end of 2001, 376 years later, he would have had a bank account of over $78 billion, if income taxes are ignored. You are invited to judge for yourself whether Peter made a wise purchase.

TABLE 1.2
Accumulation of $24 in 376 Years at 6% Compound Interest per Year

Year	Ending Balance
1626	$25
1675	$442
1725	$8,143
1775	$150,000
1825	$2,763,000
1875	$50,895,000
1925	$937,500,000
1975	$17,268,877,000
2001	$78,562,733,000

23.　But, to carry the illustration a step further, notice in table 1.2 how slowly Peter Minuit's account would have grown in the first 300 years. His money was on the flat part of the curve in figure 1.1. By 1925, he wouldn't even have become a billionaire. He really would have gotten fabulously wealthy only in the past 76 years, during which time his wealth would have grown by over $78 billion. In 2001 alone, it would have increased by about $4.4 billion! (Again, an important point to remember is that the *rate* of growth of his wealth was constant throughout the period, 6 percent per year. It is the *amount* of growth that accelerates under compound interest.)

Effect of Income Taxes

24.   One factor that must be considered in the analysis of several types of time-value-of-money problems is the impact of income taxes – federal, state, and local. For example, the rate of return nominally realized from most investments should be adjusted downward to an aftertax basis. Similarly, the nominal size of a payment or interest rate on a loan should be adjusted downward by the borrower if the payments are deductible for income tax purposes. We have not explicitly factored tax considerations into the problems discussed in this book but have, instead, implicitly assumed that all values in the problems discussed are aftertax values.

Frequency of Compounding or Discounting

25.   As you will see in the next chapter of this book, there is another factor, in addition to the interest rate and the number of years, that affects the size of the present and future values of money. That factor is the frequency with which the interest rate is applied in the compounding or discounting process.

26.   Throughout this and most of the next chapter, it will be assumed that the interest rate is applied once per year, which is called annual compounding or discounting. You should recognize, however, that in many cases, interest rates are applied several times within a year - for example, semiannually (twice per year), monthly (12 times per year), or daily (usually computed in commercial transactions by applying the interest rate 360 times per year).

27.   All other things being equal, the greater the frequency with which compounding or discounting occurs, the greater is the effect on the growth of a future value or the decline of a present value. For example, a $1,000 principal sum that is credited with 8 percent compound interest will grow to a future value of $1,166.40 in two years if compounding occurs annually. If compounding occurs semiannually, on the other hand, it will grow to $1,169.86; and if compounding occurs

monthly, it will grow to $1,172.89. Conversely, the present value of $1,000 due two years from now is $857.34 if an 8 percent annual interest rate is applied once per year. If the discounting is applied semiannually, however, the present value is only $854.80.

28.   The explanation of why the frequency of compounding or discounting produces these results and of how to compute present and future values based on various frequencies will be deferred to the next chapter. Meanwhile, unless instructed otherwise, you should assume in the text and problems in Chapters One and Two and in the practice multiple choice questions in Chapter Three that compounding and discounting occur only once per year.

Measuring the Number of Periods

29.   Before moving on, you should note one other factor to keep in mind in the compounding or discounting process. That is, the importance of being accurate in measuring the number of periods during which the compounding or discounting occurs. That, in turn, will depend on whether the process begins and ends at the beginning or the end of the periods in question.

30.   If that sounds a bit confusing, refer back to the example of Peter Minuit in table 1.2. In that illustration, year number one was 1626, and the account balance for that year was $25. That result occurred because it was assumed that $24 was deposited on January 1, 1626, the *beginning* of year one, and the account balance was computed on December 31, 1626, the *end* of year one. As a consequence, year one produced approximately $1.00 of interest.

31.   On the other hand, what if Peter had deposited the initial $24 at the *end* of year one? Obviously, the ending account balance for that year would have been $24, and no interest would have been earned in that year.

32.   The effect of this change in the assumption about when the initial deposit was made, whether at the start or the end of the first year, carries over into all remaining years. In table 1.2, the ending balance for 2001, some $78.5 billion, was the result of compounding for 376 years, that is, from January 1, 1626, to December 31, 2001. If Peter had begun his investment just 12 months later, at the end of 1626, compounding would have occurred for only 375 years by December 31, 2001, and his account balance would have been only about $74.1 billion. In other words, the 12-month delay would have cost him more than $4.4 billion of interest earnings. What a difference a year makes!

33.   Problems in which students most frequently make mistakes in measuring the period of time over which compounding or discounting takes place are those that involve a series of payments. In order to be sure you are counting n, the number of periods, accurately in solving time-value-of-money problems, it will be helpful to draw time lines such as those in figure 1.2 and to mark the timing of known dollar values in the problem with vertical arrows along the time line and the timing of unknown dollar values with question marks. The reason for drawing certain arrows below the line and others above it will be explained in a few minutes. For the present, you need only to recognize how the *timing* of each sum of money in a problem, both the known and unknown sums, is depicted on a time line. The upper time line, for example, depicts a case where you are to calculate the future value as of the beginning of the sixth period (which is the same as the end of the fifth period) of a deposit made at the beginning of the first period. The lower time line depicts a situation in which you are to compute the present value as of today (the start of period one) of a series of payments that will occur at the end of each of the next four periods. Time lines can be constructed for all types of time-value-of-money problems, as will be shown frequently throughout this chapter and the next one.

Figure 1.2
Time Lines as a Help in Counting Number of Periods of
Compounding or Discounting

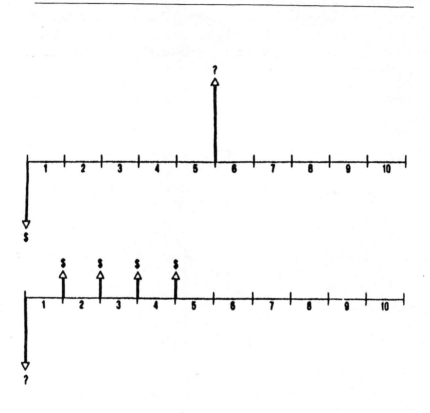

The top time line reflects a problem in which a present value is
deposited at the start of period one, and you are asked to solve
for the future value at the start of period six, or the end of period
five. The lower time line depicts a problem in which a sum of
money is to be paid at the end of each of the next four periods,
and you are asked to solve for their present value as of the start
of period one.

Plan of the Time-Value Discussion

34. The balance of this chapter utilizes and builds upon the elementary concepts presented thus far. Emphasis is placed upon explaining *how to solve* various types of basic problems involving the time value of money. The same emphasis is present in the following chapter, where somewhat more advanced and complex TVM problems are explained. Practical illustrations are used constantly to demonstrate principles and solution techniques. Review problems and their answers are presented at the end of each chapter so that you can test your mastery of each type of problem explained. Then, in Chapter Three, you will be provided with a series of multiple choice questions on topics that are frequently found on professional designation examinations for the Certified Financial Planner (CFP), Chartered Life Underwriter (CLU), Chartered Financial Consultant (ChFC), and other programs. Explanations of the answers to these multiple choice questions also are provided.

35. Although this and the following chapters deal with the interactions among numbers - dollars, interest rates, and time periods - you do not need a sophisticated knowledge of mathematics in order to perform any of the calculations. An ability to add, subtract, multiply, and divide, as well as an ability to raise a number to a power, will be helpful. Even these are not totally essential, however, if you have access to a financial calculator. (The procedure for raising a number to a power or for solving any other type of time-value-of-money problem by means of a financial calculator is described in Appendices A, B, C, and D at the end of this book.)

36. This book contains an explanation of two types of tools that can be used to solve time-value-of-money problems. At the low-tech end of the spectrum, explanations are provided for solving them by directly applying mathematical formulas to the data. A rung much higher up the technological ladder is the use of a financial calculator. Procedures for using four of the most popular electronic calculators with time-value capabilities are explained.

37. The explanation of the various types of time-value problems treated in this and the next chapter proceeds in a logical progression from the least complicated to the more advanced types. The rest of Chapter One deals with the future value and present value of single sums of money, as well as the future value and present value of level streams of money payments, called annuities. Chapter Two then takes up the future value and present value of nonlevel streams of money payments. These topics are then applied to investment decisions through an explanation of discounted cash flow analysis. Then, the assumption that compounding, discounting, and payments occur only once per year is dropped, and an explanation is provided on how to deal with any of the preceding types of problems where compounding, discounting, or payment frequency is greater than annual.

38. Now, to begin.

FUTURE VALUE OF A SINGLE SUM

39. The most frequently encountered and easiest to understand application of the time-value-of-money concept involves the future value of a single sum. As explained earlier, determination of a future value of a sum of money entails a process of compounding, or increasing. the present value at some interest rate for some period of time. The most common example is the growth of a sum placed in an interest-bearing savings account. Recall, for example, that in table 1.1, a $100 deposit made today (a present value) will grow to $133.82 (a future value) at the end of five years at 6 percent compound interest.

Basic Time-Value Formula

40. The basic formula for computing the future value of a single sum of money, from which all other time-value formulas are derived, is the following:

$$\text{FVSS} = \text{PVSS}\,(1+i)^n$$

Where:

FVSS	=	Future value of a single sum
PVSS	=	Present value of a single sum
i	=	Compound periodic interest rate, expressed as a decimal
n	=	Number of periods during which compounding occurs

That is, add the interest rate (expressed as a decimal) to one and raise this sum to a power equal to the number of periods during which the compounding occurs. Then, multiply this by the present value of the single sum or deposit in question to compute the future value of that single sum.

41.   For example, assume that $5,000 is placed on deposit today in an account that will earn 9 percent compound annual interest. To what amount will this sum of money grow by the end of year seven? The problem is depicted on a time line in figure 1.3 below.

Figure 1.3
Time Line Depiction of FVSS Problem

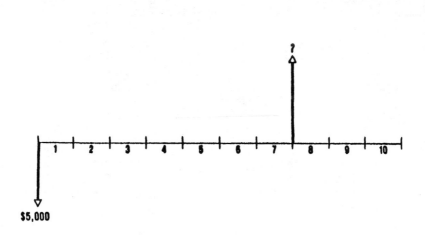

This time line depicts a problem in which a known single sum, $5,000, is deposited today, at the start of year one, and you are to calculate its future value as of the end of year seven. The time line also illustrates the basic trade-off present in all time-value-of-money problems. Here, the trade-off is a cash outflow today (the deposit, shown below the time line) for a larger cash inflow later (the account balance at the end of the seventh year, shown above the time line).

---

42.   It is important, both conceptually and mathematically, to recognize that in every time-value-of-money problem, there is an implicit trade-off over time of a sacrifice for a gain, a cost for a benefit. For example, you may be willing to loan money to a friend today (a cost or cash outflow in the present) in order to be repaid a larger amount later (a benefit or larger cash inflow in the

future). Throughout the time-value-of-money discussions in this book, the nature of this trade-off will be pointed out over and over. For purposes of consistency among the time lines used to depict various types of problems to be discussed, present values will be depicted below the line, as will periodic cash outflows. Future values and periodic cash inflows will be shown as above-the-line factors.

43.   To return to the problem at hand, then, the $5,000 that is placed on deposit today represents a present value. The amount to which it will grow at 9 percent compound annual interest by the end of the seventh year is the future value. The basic time value formula can be used to compute the solution as follows:

$$
\begin{aligned}
FVSS &= PVSS\ (1 + i)^n \\
&= \$5,000\ (1.09)^7 \\
&= \$5,000\ (1.828039) \\
&= \$9,140.20
\end{aligned}
$$

44.   To reiterate a point made earlier in this chapter, note what would happen to FVSS if i were more than 9 percent or if n were more than seven years. In either case, the quantity $(1 + i)^n$ would be larger than 1.828039, so that when multiplied by $5,000, the FVSS would be larger than $9,140.20. That is, the future value increases as the interest rate or the number of periods increases, and it falls as either of them is reduced.

Computing FVSS With a Calculator With Finance Functions

45.   A powerful tool for solving time-value-of-money problems is the financial calculator. This type of calculator greatly speeds the task of solving these problems, especially the more complex ones described later. Four of the most popular electronic calculators with finance functions currently on the market are the HP-12C Programmable Financial Calculator, the HP-17B II Financial (Business) Calculator, the HP-10B II Financial Calculator, all produced by Hewlett-Packard Company, and the BA-II Plus calculator produced by Texas Instruments Incorporated. In this book, an explanation will be

furnished, showing how to solve on these four calculators each type of time-value-of-money problem as it is encountered.[2] The individual keystrokes in each sequence of calculator keystrokes shown are separated by commas. If at some point in a sequence you key in an incorrect number, you can correct the mistake by immediately pressing the CLX key on the HP-12C, the left arrow key on the HP-17B II or HP-10B II calculator, or the right arrow key on the BA-II Plus.

Using the HP-12C

46.   To use the HP-12C calculator to solve future value of a single sum problems, turn the machine on by pressing the ON key in the lower left corner of the keyboard. Next, depress the yellow f key[3] and the CLX key, which has REG printed above it. This serves to clear any data that may have been stored earlier in the financial and several other "registers" (memory units) of the machine. If you wish to clear only the financial registers, press the yellow f key and the xy key, which has FIN printed above it, instead. (It is a very good idea to get into the habit of clearing the memory of the calculator each time you use it to solve a problem.) Next, depress the yellow f key and the number 2. This will cause the machine to display dollar values carried to two decimal places, which is the level of precision to be used for dollar values throughout most of this book. (As will be explained later, other values, such as those for an interest rate, will sometimes be entered or displayed with other numbers of decimal places.)

47.   By the way, what you have just done affects only the number of decimal places *displayed*. In most calculations, it does not have any impact on the precision with which the machine performs the actual calculations.

48.   The next steps are to enter the three known values in the FVSS problem, namely, PVSS, n, and i. These may be entered in any order. The language of the HP-12C, however, includes an important convention that reflects the cost-benefit trade-off in all time-value problems referred to earlier. This convention, called

the cash flow sign convention, requires that at least one (and usually only one) value entered into the calculator in a time-value problem be entered as a negative number. This is accomplished through use of the CHS (change sign) key in the top row of the keyboard. If this is not done, the cash flow sign convention usually causes solutions to problems to be displayed as negative numbers. For purposes of consistency, *present values* will be entered or displayed as negative numbers. Also, as will be explained later, the amount of a payment that constitutes a cash *outflow* in a series of payments in some types of problems will be entered or displayed as a negative number on the HP-12C.

49. Now take a moment to review the keys in the left-hand portion of the top row of the keyboard. These keys (n, i, PV, PMT, and FV), as well as the yellow and blue functions they activate and the CHS key, will be used in solving various types of time-value-of-money problems.

50. To return to the example given earlier, assume that you wish to know the amount to which a single sum of $5,000 will grow in seven years at 9 percent compound interest. Since i is 9, press the 9 key, then the i key. Since n is 7, depress 7, then n. And since the sum of money today is $5,000, press 5000, CHS (since it is the present value), and PV. Finally, press FV, and the answer, $9,140.20, will appear on the display.[4]

51. If you wish to change one of the data items in the problem, you may do so without reentering all the information. For example, if you wish to recalculate the same problem with a 12 percent interest rate, before clearing the machine, simply press 12, i, and FV. The new amount, $11,053.41, appears on the display.

Using the HP-10B II

52. To use the HP-10B II to solve TVM problems, turn the machine on by pressing the ON key in the lower left-hand corner of the keyboard. Then, you need to take care of several

housekeeping tasks. Press the orange shift key, which is two keys above the ON key, and the C key, which has C ALL printed below it.[5] This serves to clear any data that may have been stored earlier in any of the calculator's memory registers. (It is a very good idea to get into the habit of doing this every time you turn on the machine since "trash" left over from an earlier problem may cause an incorrect answer to the problem you want to work on now.) Next, press the orange shift key and the = key, which has DISP printed below it. Press the 2 or 4 key to specify the number of decimal places to be displayed. Two decimal places are what we will use for dollar values, though sometimes we will want to display four decimal places, for example, in some interest rate calculations.

53.   By the way, what you have just done affects only the number of decimal places *displayed*. It does not affect the precision with which the machine performs calculations.

54.   Another *very* important housekeeping chore is to set the HP-10B II for one payment period and one compounding period per year. In Chapter Two we will take up problems in which more than one payment or compounding period occurs in a year, but for now let's keep life simple. Press 1, shift, and PMT (which has P/YR printed below it. Press shift and C ALL to lock this in place. Do not change this setting – ever – except for the case dealt with in Para. 153 of Chapter Two!

55.   Now that the housekeeping chores are done, you won't need to do them again (except to clear the machine after/before every problem). So, now we'll proceed to calculate the future value of a single sum. This requires that we enter the three known values in the FVSS problem, namely, the present value of the single sum (PV), the number of periods (N), and the interest rate per year (I/YR). These may be done in any order. However, you must remember the cost-benefit trade-off found in every TVM problem that we mentioned earlier. Entering a number as a negative is accomplished through the use of the +/- key in the left-hand column of the keyboard. For purposes of consistency, we will enter or display *present values* as negative numbers.

Also, later on, we will take up problems involving periodic cash flows in or out. Periodic *outflows* will also be entered or displayed as negative numbers.

56.   Take a moment to review the top row of the keyboard. The first five keys there (N, I/YR, PV, PMT, and FV), as well as the +/- key and, later, the shift key will be used to solve various. types of TVM problems.

57.   To return to the example given earlier, assume that you want to know the amount to which a single sum of $5,000 will grow in seven years at 9 percent compound annual interest. Since $5,000 is the sum today, press 5000, +/- (because it is the present value), and PV. Then, press 9 and I/YR because 9 percent is the compound annual interest rate. Finally, press 7, N (because seven is the number of periods in the problem), and FV (which is the value to be calculated). The answer, $9,140.20, will appear on the display.[6]

58.   If you want to change one of the data items in the problem, you may do so without reentering all the information. For example, if you want to recalculate the same problem with an 8 percent interest rate, before clearing the machine, simply press 8, I/YR, and FV. The new amount, $8,569.12, appears on the display.

Using the HP-17B II

59.   If you are using the HP-17B II to solve TVM problems, you should first take care of a number of housekeeping chores. Turn the machine on by pressing the CLR key in the lower left corner of the keyboard. Turn it off by pressing the colored shift key[7] just above it and then the CLR key again. (Note that OFF is printed in color above the CLR key.) Now adjust the contrast level on the display screen to one that is comfortable for you. Do this by holding down the CLR key and pressing the + key or the – key several times. Next, select the Algebraic system of entry logic by pressing shift and MODES on the DSP key. Now press the menu key, the key labelled ∧, that is directly below

ALG on the screen. Then, press the EXIT key in the upper right portion of the keyboard. Do not change this setting – ever!

60.   Next, set the number of decimal places to be displayed on the screen. We will use two decimal places for most dollar values in this book, so press DSP, the menu (∧) key under FIX, then 2, and the INPUT key in the upper left portion of the keyboard. (In some cases, such as when dealing with large dollar amounts, we will display figures with no decimal places. In other cases, such as when calculating an interest rate, we may use four decimal places.)

61.   By the way, the setting for the number of decimal places applies only to what appears on the display. It does not normally affect the precision with which the machine performs actual calculations.

62.   Of *extreme* importance as a housekeeping chore, you should set the HP-17B II for one payment period per year and one compounding period per year. In Chapter Two we will take up problems in which more than one payment or compounding period occurs in a year, but for now, we will keep life simple. Press shift, MAIN on the EXIT key, the FIN menu key, the TVM menu key, the OTHER menu key, 1, the P/YR menu key, shift, MAIN, and CLR. Do not change this setting – ever!

63.   One more important housekeeping chore that should be performed before every time-value problem is taken up is to clear the calculator of any data left in it from a previous problem. To do this, press shift, MAIN, the FIN menu key, shift, CLEAR DATA on the INPUT key, shift, and MAIN. Get into this habit every time you turn the calculator on and every time you wish to solve a new problem. Otherwise, you may produce incorrect results for the problem.

64.   Now that all of the housekeeping has been taken care of, you will not need to do it again (except to clear the machine). The various settings will remain in the machine continuously, unless and until you specifically change them. So let's proceed

to compute the future value of a single sum. Turn the machine on and press shift and MAIN. On the display screen you will see the calculator's main memory system. We will use only the finance menu system, so press the FIN menu key. The next level of the menu shows TVM, ICNV, CFLO, BOND, and DEPRC. In this chapter we will use only the TVM functions, so press the TVM menu key.

65.   The next steps are to enter the three known values in the FVSS problem into the calculator. In doing so, it is important to remember the cost-benefit trade-off present in all TVM problems as was explained earlier. Entering a number as a negative is accomplished through the use of the +/- key, which is located next to the INPUT key. For purposes of consistency, *present values* will be entered or displayed as negative numbers. Also, as will be explained later, the amount of a payment that constitutes a cash *outflow* in a series of payments in some types of problems will be entered or displayed as a negative number.

66.   Now take a moment to review the TVM menu. The display shows one payment per year, which we entered earlier, and either END MODE or BEGIN MODE. We can ignore these modes for now, as they will not affect the calculations to be performed in this chapter. The display also shows the labels N, I%YR, PV, PMT, FV, and OTHER. The menu keys for these labels will be used to solve many types of TVM problems.

67.   To return to the example given earlier, assume that you wish to know the amount to which a single sum of $5,000 will grow in seven years at 9 percent compound interest. Since the number of periods is 7, depress 7, then the N menu key. Since the interest rate is 9, press the 9 key, then the I%YR menu key. And since the sum of money today is $5,000, press 5000, the +/- key (since it is a present value), and the PV menu key. Finally, press the FV menu key, and the answer, $9,140.20, will appear on the display.[8]

68.   If you wish to change one or two of the data items in the problem, you may do so without reentering all the information.

For example, if you wish to recalculate the same problem with a 12 percent interest, simply press, 12, the I%YR menu key, and the FV menu key. The new answer, $11,053.41, will appear on the display.

Using the BA-II Plus

69. In order to solve time-value-of-money problems using the BA-II Plus calculator, turn the machine on and clear the display screen by pressing the ON/OFF key in the upper right-hand corner of the keyboard. Next, clear the calculator of any previous information contained in the calculator's memory units. This is accomplished by pressing the grey key labeled 2nd near the upper left-hand corner[9] and the number 0 key, which has MEM printed above it. Then press 2nd and the FV key, which has CLR TVM printed above it. Then to complete the task, press 2nd again, followed by the CE/C key with CLR Work printed above it. (It is a very good idea to get into the habit of clearing the memory of the calculator each time you use it to solve a problem.) Next press 2nd, the decimal point key with Format printed above it, and the number 2 key. Then press ENTER, 2nd, and QUIT, which is printed above the CPT key. This will cause the machine to display numbers rounded to two decimal places, which is the level of precision we will normally use for dollar values. (As will be explained later, other values, such as those for interest rates, will sometimes be entered or displayed with other numbers of decimal places.)

70. By the way, what you have just done affects only the number of decimal places *displayed*. In most calculations, it does not have any impact on the precision with which the machine performs the actual calculations.

71. Another *very* important housekeeping function is to set the BA-II Plus for one payment per year and one compounding period per year. In Chapter Two we will take up problems in which more than one payment or compounding period occurs in a year, but for now, we will keep life simple. Press 2nd and the I/Y key, which has P/Y printed above it, in the third row of the

keyboard from the top. Then press 1, the ENTER key in the top row, the 2nd key again, and the QUIT function on the CPT key in the top left corner. Do not change this setting – ever!

72.   Now that all the housekeeping has been taken care of, you will not need to do it again (except to clear the machine). The various settings will remain in the machine continuously, unless and until you specifically change them. So let's proceed to compute the future value of a single sum.

73.   The BA-II Plus uses two modes for solving the problems we will be discussing: the standard-calculator mode (which is used for routine arithmetic and for most basic time-value-of-money problems) and the prompted-worksheet mode (which is used to solve some advanced problems we will discuss later). For now, put the machine in the standard-calculator mode by pressing 2nd followed by the CPT key that has QUIT printed above it.

74.   Take a moment to review the keys in the third row from the top of the keyboard. These keys (N, I/Y, PV, PMT, and FV), along with the 2nd key and the CPT (compute) and ENTER keys in the top row, will be used in solving various types of time-value-of-money problems.

75.   The language of the BA-II Plus includes an important convention that reflects the cost-benefit trade-off inherent in all time-value problems as described earlier. This convention requires that at least one (and usually only one) value entered into the calculator in a time-value problem be entered as a negative number. This is accomplished through the use of the +/- key in the bottom row of the keyboard. For consistency, *present values* will be entered or displayed as negative numbers. As will be explained later, the amount of a payment that constitutes a cash *outflow* in a series of payments in some types of problems will also be entered or displayed as a negative number on the BA-II Plus.

76.   To return to the example given earlier, assume you wish to know the amount to which a single sum of $5,000 will grow in seven years at 9 percent compound interest. These three known values should be entered into the calculator. They may be entered in any order. Since the interest rate per year is 9 percent, press 9 and I/Y. Then enter the number of years involved by pressing 7 and N. Next is the sum of money today. Press 5000, +/- (to change it to a negative value because it is a present value), and PV. Finally, press CPT and FV and the answer, $9,140.20, appears on the display.[10]

77.   If you wish to change one of the data items in the problem, you may do so without reentering all the information. For example, if you wish to recalculate the same problem with a five-year compounding period, before clearing the machine, simply press 5, N, CPT, and FV. The new amount, $7,693.12, appears on the display.

Rule of 72

78.   Occasionally, you may find it unnecessary to obtain a precise measurement of the effect of interest in the compounding process and that a rough estimate of the future value of a single sum will suffice. In such cases, a simple device called the "rule of 72" may be found useful.

79.   The rule of 72 is a quick method for estimating how long it will take for a sum to double in value at various compound interest rates. In this method, the number 72 is divided by the applicable interest rate expressed as a whole number. The quotient is the number of periods in question.[11]

80.   For example, at a compound annual interest rate of 9 percent, a $100 principal sum will double in value and reach $200 in approximately (72 ÷ 9 =) eight years. It will double again and reach $400 in approximately another eight years and double still again, reaching $800, at the end of approximately eight more years. At a compound annual interest rate of 6 percent, on the other hand, the growth of the principal sum will

be much slower since it will take about (72 ÷ 6 =) 12 years for each doubling to occur.

81.   Remember that the rule of 72 produces only approximations, and that for most purposes, you will want to be more precise. Moreover, the amount of imprecision produced by using the rule of 72 increases as the interest rate and the principal sum are increased. (As a partial corrective measure, some prefer to divide the interest rate into the number 78 for interest rates of 20 percent or more.) More precise methods for computing the effects of compounding than the rules of 72 or 78 will be used in the balance of this book.

Computing n or i

82.   In some types of future value of a single-sum problems, FVSS and PVSS are known, as well as either i or n. The task in such cases is to use the three known valucs to compute the fourth.

83.   For example, assume that you plan to deposit $1,200 in a savings account and withdraw the money when the account balance reaches $1,500. How long will you have to wait if the annual compound interest rate on the account is 7.5 percent?

84.   The reader who is mathematically talented can solve this problem through the basic time-value formula by substituting the known values in it as shown below and then solving for n.[12]

$$1500 = 1200 \, (1.075)^n$$

85.   It should be obvious that the formula doesn't provide a quick and precise method for dealing with the problem of computing n. An electronic calculator with finance functions, however, can compute n as readily as it computes FVSS.

86.   On the HP-12C, for example, after clearing the machine as described above, enter the three known values in any order and solve for the fourth. Press 7.5, i, 1500, FV, 1200, CHS (in

accordance with the machine's cash flow sign convention), PV, and n. The answer, 4.00 years, appears on the display.

87.   Actually, this is an incomplete answer because of a design limitation of the HP-12C in dealing with the calculation of n. If the answer is not an integer, or whole number, the HP-12C usually rounds the answer up to the next higher integer. This, in effect, means that the final period contained in the displayed value for n is actually only a partial period. (The HP-12C rounds down to the next lower integer if the portion of n to the right of the decimal point is less than .005, resulting in a slight understatement of the actual n.)   If you wish a more precise value for n on the HP-12C, the best approach is to use the formula in note 12 at the end of this chapter, together with the log function of the calculator.

88.   The HP-10B II, the HP-17B II, and the BA-II Plus provide a more precise answer to the problem of computing the number of periods than does the HP-12C. If you are using the HP-10B II, set the calculator to display, say, four decimal places. Clear the machine and press 7.5, I/YR, 1500, FV, 1200, +/-, PV, and N. The answer, 3.0855 years, will be displayed.

89.   If you are using the HP-17B II, set the calculator to display, say, four decimal places. Then go to the TVM menu system and clear its memory. Then use the menu keys to enter 7.5 as I%YR, 1200 as a negative PV, and 1500 as FV. Press the N menu key and the answer, 3.0855 years, will be displayed.

90.   If, instead, you are using the BA-II Plus, after clearing the machine's display and memory and setting it for, for example, four decimal places as described earlier, press 7.5, I/Y, 1500, FV, 1200, +/-, PV, CPT, and N. The answer, 3.0855 years, appears on the display.

91.   Instead of solving for n or N in a time-value problem, in many cases, the task will be to solve for the interest rate. For example, what compound annual interest rate must you earn on your money if you have $6,000 to invest today and wish to have

$10,000 in five years? Solving this type of problem is complex mathematically. Hence, an explanation involving the use of a formula will not be attempted here. Convenience and precision in solving for i, however, are possible with a financial calculator.

92. On the HP-12C, for example, set the number of decimal places to four and enter the three known values in any order: 10000, FV, 5, n, 6000, CHS, PV, and i. After a few seconds, the answer appears as 10.7566 percent.

93. On the HP-10B II, set the calculator for four decimal places and clear the machine. Then press 10000, FV, 5, N, 6000, +/-, PV, and I/YR. The answer, 10.7566 percent, will be displayed.

94. On the HP-17B II, with the calculator displaying four decimal places, clear the TVM memory and use the menu keys to enter 5, N, 6000, +/-, PV, 10000, FV, and I%YR. The answer will appear as 10.7566%.

95. Or on the BA-II Plus, after you make sure the memory is clear, set the number of decimal places to four and press 5, N, 6000, +/-, PV, 10000, FV, CPT, and I/Y to produce the answer, 10.7566 percent. (As with the HP-12C, any order in which you choose to enter the three known variables on the other three calculators is acceptable.)

PRESENT VALUE OF A SINGLE SUM

96. The preceding pages dealt with the question of compounding, of computing how a known single sum of money accumulates over time to an unknown future value. Now the question will be reversed. Given the future value of a single sum of money, what is it worth today? What is its present, or discounted, value?

97. For example, assume that in four years, it will be necessary to spend $125,000 to replace an asset that is wearing out. How much money should be on hand today in an account

earning 10 percent compound annual interest in order to reach that goal? Or, assume that you are scheduled to receive a $75,000 lump-sum distribution from a trust five years from now. For how much would you sell that right today (if you are permitted to do so) if interest rates are 7 percent? (See figure 1.4.)

Figure 1.4
Time Line Representation of PVSS Problems

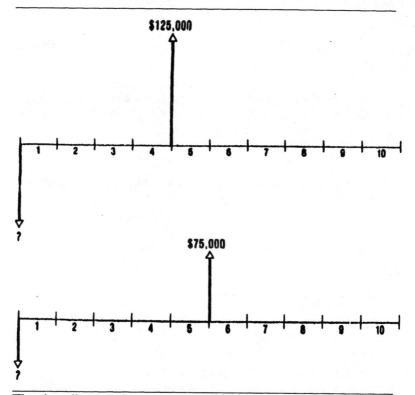

The time line on the top represents a problem in which you are asked to determine the present value of a $125,000 single sum due four years hence. In the time line on the bottom, the problem is to compute the PVSS when the FVSS is $75,000 due in five years.

38

Using the Time-Value Formula

98.   You learned earlier that FVSS can be found through the formula:

$$FVSS = PVSS (1+i)^n$$

Students of elementary algebra will recognize that this formula can be rearranged to:

$$PVSS = FVSS \left[\frac{1}{(1+i)^n}\right] = \frac{FVSS}{(1+i)^n}$$

That is, FVSS multiplied by the mathematical reciprocal of $(1+i)^n$, which is the same as dividing FVSS by $(1+i)^n$, produces the PVSS. Discounting is thus the reverse of compounding. When compounding, you should multiply the known sum by $(1+i)^n$, whereas in discounting, you should multiply it by the reciprocal of that quantity (or divide it by that quantity).

99.   In the top line of figure 1.4, then, you need to have $125,000 in four years for replacement of the wearing-out asset. If you can earn 10 percent compound interest, you should set aside today a total of a little over $85,000. That is:

$$PVSS = \$125,000 \left[\frac{1}{(1.10)^4}\right] = \frac{\$125,000}{(1.10)^4}$$

$$= \frac{\$125,000}{1.4641}$$

$$= \$85,376.68$$

This amount, accumulating at 10 percent compound annual interest, will grow to the necessary $125,000 when it is needed in four years.

100.   And, the present value of that $75,000 trust fund distribution due to be received in five years, if the interest rate is 7 percent, is a little more than $53,000.

$$\text{PVSS} = \$75,000 \left[\frac{1}{(1.07)^5}\right] = \frac{\$75,000}{(1.07)^5}$$

$$= \frac{\$75,000}{1.4026}$$

$$= \$53,472.12$$

101.   Note the effect of a change in i or n on PVSS. If either of these is increased, the denominator of the formula increases and, when it is divided into FVSS, the resulting PVSS declines. For example, the present value of the $75,000 trust fund distribution due in five years is only $46,569.39 if the interest rate used in discounting is 10 percent; it is still smaller, $34,987.87, if it is due in eight years and the interest rate is 10 percent. A decrease in either i or n, on the other hand, causes PVSS to rise.

102.   The calculation of present values by means of the formula is as tedious, time-consuming, and susceptible to errors as is the calculation of future values. To simplify the process of computing PVSS, a financial calculator is highly recommended.

Computing PVSS with a Financial Calculator

Using the HP-12C

103.   If you are using the HP-12C financial calculator, as explained earlier, clear the machine and set it to display two decimal places. The next step is to enter the three known values into the machine in any order. Then press the PV button to solve for the present value of the single sum in question.

104.   For example, assume that you own a zero-coupon bond that will mature in 13 years, at which time it will pay you $1,000. Meanwhile, it will pay you nothing. What would you sell the bond for today, as a minimum, if you believe you could invest the proceeds elsewhere and earn 9 percent compound interest?

105.   Enter 9, i, 13, n, 1000, and FV. The calculator is now programmed to compute the present value of the $1,000 due to be received in the future. Depress the PV key and the answer,

$326.18, is displayed. (Remember that the HP-12C's cash flow sign convention referred to earlier shows the answer as a negative number if all the data are entered as positive numbers.) That is, if you were to invest $326.18 at 9 percent compound interest, you would have $1,000 at the end of 13 years. (You may wish to verify this by computing the FVSS of $326.18, as explained earlier in this chapter.)

Using the HP-10B II

106.   If you are using the HP-10B II calculator to compute the present value of a single sum, clear the memory and set the machine to display two decimal places as explained earlier. Then enter the three known variables in any order and solve for PV.

107.   For example, assume that you own a zero-coupon bond that will mature in six years for $1,000. Meanwhile, it will pay you nothing. What would you sell the bond for today, as a minimum, if you believe you could invest the proceeds elsewhere and earn 9 3/4 percent compound annual interest?

108.   Press 1000, FV, 6, N, 9.75, I/YR, and PV. The answer is $572.23. (This answer will be displayed as a negative number because the other three variables were entered as positive numbers – the cost/benefit trade-off.) That is, if you were to invest $572.23 today at 9 3/4 percent compound annual interest, you would have $1,000 at the end of six years. (You may wish to verify this by computing the FVSS of $572.23, as explained earlier in this chapter.)

Using the HP-17B II

109.   If you wish to use the HP-17B II to compute the present value of a single sum, set the calculator to display two decimal places. Clear the TVM menu system's memory. Then enter the three known variables in the problem by pressing the appropriate menu keys. Lastly, press the PV menu key to produce the answer.

110.   For example, assume that you own a zero-coupon bond that will mature in 15 years for $1,000. Meanwhile, it will pay you nothing. What would you sell the bond for today, as a

minimum, if you believe you could invest the proceeds elsewhere and earn 8 1/2 percent compound interest?

111.   Enter 15 as the N, 8.5 as the I%YR, and 1000 as the FV. Press the PV menu key to find the answer, and $294.14 will be displayed. (Remember that present values are displayed as negative numbers because the three known variables were all entered as positive numbers.) That is, if you were to invest $294.14 at 8.5 percent compound interest, you would have $1,000 at the end of 15 years. (You may wish to verify this by computing the FVSS of $294.14 as explained earlier in this chapter.)

Using the BA-II Plus

112.   If you wish to use the BA-II Plus calculator to compute the present value of a single sum, clear the memory and set the machine to display two decimal places, as was explained earlier. Then, enter the three known values into the calculator in any order. Finally, press the CPT and PV keys to compute the present value of the single sum in question.

113.   For example, assume that you own a zero-coupon bond that will mature in six years, at which time it will pay you $1,000. Meanwhile, it will pay you nothing. What would you sell the bond for today, as a minimum, if you believe you could invest the proceeds elsewhere and earn 11 percent compound interest?

114.   Enter 1000, FV, 11, I/Y, 6, and N. The calculator is now programmed to compute the present value of the $1,000 due to be received in the future. Depress the CPT and PV keys and the answer, $534.64, is displayed. (Remember that the BA-II Plus shows the present value as a negative number if all the data are entered as positive numbers.) That is, if you were to invest $534.64 at 11 percent compound interest for the next six years, you would have $1,000 at the end of that time. (You may wish to verify this by computing the FVSS of $534.64 as explained earlier in this chapter.)

Rule of 72

115.   Earlier in this chapter, the rule of 72 was presented as a quick method for estimating how long it will take for a sum of money to double in value. The rule can also be used to estimate how long it will take for a sum of money to halve in value. For example, if an average annual inflation rate of 8 percent should be experienced over an extended period, a person's $50,000 salary would fall in purchasing power to $25,000 in approximately (72 ÷ 8 =) nine years (if the salary remains at $50,000).

Computing n or i

116.   As is true of future value problems, it is sometimes useful to be able to compute either n or i, given the other and given FVSS and PVSS. For example, assume that you owe $5,000 to be paid in a lump sum in two years. The lender offers to accept $4,750 today in satisfaction of the loan. Should you accept the offer? The answer depends at least partly on the rate of return (interest) the lender is effectively offering you.

117.   You can use a financial calculator to find the answer. Set your HP-12C to display four decimal places. Then enter 5000, FV, 4750, CHS (again, present values should be entered as negative numbers), PV, 2, and n. Then press the i key to produce the answer, 2.5978 percent.

118.   Or, set your HP-10B II to display four decimal places. Then press 2, N, 5000, FV, 4750, +/-, PV (again, present vlaues should be entered as negative numbers), and I/YR. The answer is 2.5978 percent.

119.   Or, set your HP-17B II to display four decimal places. Then press 2, the N menu key, 4750, +/- (because it is a present value), the PV menu key, 5000, the FV menu key, and the I%YR menu key. The answer is 2.5978 percent, the rate of return you would realize by paying off the loan today.

120.   Or, set your BA-II Plus to display four decimal places. Then press 2, N, 4750, +/- (again, present values should be entered as negative numbers), PV, 5000, and FV. Then depress the CPT and I/Y keys. The lender has offered you a compound annual rate of return on your money of 2.5978 percent.

121.   To reverse this illustration, if you insist on obtaining an 8 percent compound annual rate of return on your money, when would you be willing to pay the lender $4,750 to discharge your $5,000 debt? As was explained earlier, the HP-12C provides only an approximate answer to this type of problem. Press 4750, CHS, PV, 5000, FV, 8, i, and n to produce the answer, one year. The HP-10B, the HP-17B II, and the BA-II Plus are more precise.

122.   Set the HP-10B II to display four decimal places. Then clear the machine and press 8, I/YR, 4750, +/-, PV, 5000, FV, and N to produce the answer, 0.6665 years.

123.   Or, set the HP-17B II to display four decimal places. As always, clear the TVM menu. Then enter 8 as the I%YR, 4750 as the negative PV, and 5000 as the FV. Press the N menu key to produce the answer, 0.6665 years.

124.   Or, set the BA-II Plus to display four decimal places. Then press 8, I/Y, 4750, +/-, PV, 5000, and FV. Now press CPT and N to compute the answer, 0.6665. That is, if you repay the $5,000 loan about eight months early (two-thirds of one year) for $4,750, your compound annual rate of return will be 8 percent.

FUTURE VALUE OF AN ANNUITY OR ANNUITY DUE

125.   Earlier in this chapter we explained how to compute the future value of a *single* sum placed on deposit or paid into an account credited with compound interest. Now we will build upon and expand that case to deal with the calculation of the future value of a *series* of deposits or payments. For example, if $300 is deposited, or paid, into an account *each year* and is credited with 11 percent compound annual interest, how much will be in the account at the end of six years?

126.   This type of problem will be referred to as a future value of an annuity (FVA) or a future value of an annuity due (FVAD) problem. An annuity, sometimes called an ordinary annuity, is a series of payments of equal amounts made at the *end* of each of a number of periods. An annuity due is a series of payments of equal amounts made at the *beginning* of each of a number of periods.[13]

127.   There are many personal and business situations where sums of money are invested periodically. Some corporations, for example, make available payroll deduction plans whereby employees may save for a desired objective by having a stipulated amount withheld from each paycheck and invested in U.S. government savings bonds. Many individuals deposit a pre-established amount each week or month in banks or credit unions to save up for a vacation or for Christmas purchases. Many wage earners and self-employed individuals deposit funds each year in Individual Retirement Accounts (IRAs) or Keogh plans at banks, thrift institutions, brokerage firms, insurance companies, or mutual funds. Tax-advantaged employee benefit programs such as 401(k) and tax-deferred annuity plans are vehicles for employees to make periodic deposits, often matched by employer contributions, to save for retirement. Corporate sinking fund contributions to accumulate money for the purchase of fixed assets are another example of the annuity principle.

Assumptions

128.   To simplify the solution of FVA and FVAD problems, it will be assumed for now that the deposits or payments are made annually. This assumption will be modified in the next chapter. Also, it will be assumed that the deposits all earn the same rate of compound interest, though, obviously, each earns it for a different length of time.

129.   In that connection, it is particularly important in annuity problems to be accurate in measuring the length of time during which each deposit earns compound interest. One possible assumption is that the deposits are made at the beginning of each year (an annuity due); the other is that they are made at the end of each year (an annuity). The difference between the two future values, all other things being equal, can be quite large.

130.   For example, assume that five annual payments of $1,000 each earn 7 percent compound interest. At the end of the fifth year, the future value of these periodic payments will be $6,153.29 if they are made at the beginning of each year versus only $5,750.74 if they are made at the end.

131.   The $402.55 difference between the foregoing two future values, FVAD and FVA, is due to the fact that each deposit earns one more year of interest under the first assumption

than under the second. That is, when deposits are made at the start of each year, the first deposit earns interest for five years rather than four, the second for four years rather than three, etc., and the last deposit earns interest for one year rather than none. (See figure 1.5.)

Figure 1.5
Time Line Representation of FVAD and FVA Problems

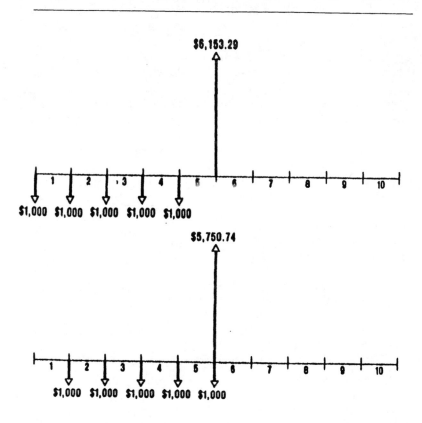

The top time line depicts a problem in which $1,000 deposits are made at the beginning of each of five years (an annuity due), and the problem is to determine the future value as of the end of the fifth year. In the lower time line, the problem is the same in all respects, except that the deposits are made at the end of each of the five years (an annuity).

Using a Time-Value Formula

132.   Problems calling for calculation of the future value of an annuity or annuity due can be viewed as collections of FVSS problems. Each annuity payment or deposit is a single sum that earns compound interest for a different number of years. Hence, the FVA or FVAD is really the sum of a series of FVSS calculations.

133.   To illustrate, assume that $100 is deposited at the end of each of four years and earns 5 percent compound annual interest. What is the total future value of these deposits at the end of the fourth year? The first deposit earns interest for three years (that is, from the end of year one till the end of year four). Hence, its future value is:

$$
\begin{aligned}
\text{FVSS} &= \text{PVSS} & (1+i)^n \\
&= \$100 & (1.05)^3 \\
&= \$100 & (1.1576) \\
&= \$115.76 &
\end{aligned}
$$

The future value of the second deposit, which earns interest for two years, is:

$$
\begin{aligned}
\text{FVSS} &= \text{PVSS} & (1+i)^n \\
&= \$100 & (1.05)^2 \\
&= \$100 & (1.1025) \\
&= \$110.25 &
\end{aligned}
$$

The future value of the third deposit, which earns interest for one year, is:

$$
\begin{aligned}
\text{FVSS} &= \text{PVSS} & (1+i)^n \\
&= \$100 & (1.05)^1 \\
&= \$105.00 &
\end{aligned}
$$

And, the future value of the fourth deposit is $100, the same as its present value, because it earns no interest. Thus, the

FVA in this illustration is ($115.76 + $110.25 + $105.00 + $100.00 =) $431.01.

134. If, on the other hand, the deposits had been made at the beginning of each year, their future values would have been as follows:

1st	$100	$(1.05)^4$	=	$121.55
2nd	$100	$(1.05)^3$	=	115.76
3rd	$100	$(1.05)^2$	=	110.25
4th	$100	$(1.05)^1$	=	105.00
		FVAD		$452.56

135. As an alternative to the foregoing approach of summing the future value of each of the separate deposits, the same result can be achieved in one step by using a somewhat more complex formula for cases where the deposits are made at the end of each year.

$$\text{FVA} = \left[\frac{(1+i)^n - 1}{i} \right] \text{(amount of one deposit)}$$

In the previous illustration:

$$\text{FVA} = \left[\frac{(1.05)^4 - 1}{.05} \right] (\$100)$$

$$= \left[\frac{.2155}{.05} \right] (\$100)$$

$$= \$431.01$$

136. For cases in which the deposits are made at the beginning of each year, the same formula may be used, but with one important modification. To reflect the fact that each deposit will be credited with one extra year of interest, it is necessary to multiply the result of the preceding formula by $(1 + i)$. That is, if deposits are made at the beginning of each year, the formula becomes:

$$\text{FVAD} \quad = \quad (1+i) \left[\frac{(1+i)^n - 1}{i} \right] \text{(amount of one deposit)}$$

$$= \quad (1.05) \left[\frac{(1.05)^4 - 1}{.05} \right] \quad (\$100)$$

$$= \quad (1.05) \left[\frac{.2155}{.05} \right] \quad (\$100)$$

$$= \quad (1.05) \, (\$431.01)$$

$$= \quad \$452.56$$

A simple way to keep the FVAD calculation in mind is to calculate FVA through the end-of-year formula above. If the problem is a beginning-of-year case, multiply the result by (1+i) to produce the FVAD.

Using a Financial Calculator To Compute FVA and FVAD

137.   As with the types of time-value problems discussed earlier in this chapter, an electronic calculator with finance functions is a very useful tool for solving FVA and FVAD problems. Among the advantages of the calculator over formulas are its great speed and its reduced likelihood of error.

Using the HP-12C

138.   To use the HP-12C, clear the memory units and set the calculator to display two decimal places. In annuity and annuity due problems, you will be using a new key on the top row of the keyboard, PMT, to reflect the fact that a series of deposits or payments is involved, rather than a single sum. Also, when solving a problem involving a series of payments or deposits, you must *always* remember to instruct the calculator as to whether the payments or deposits will be made at the end of each period (FVA) or at the beginning (FVAD). This will be accomplished through use of the blue g key and the blue END or blue BEG function in the top row of the keyboard.

139.   To illustrate, assume that a young couple deposits $5,000 today and again at the start of each of the next four years

in a savings account to accumulate a down payment for a house. If the account is credited with 8 percent compound interest per year, how much of a down payment will the couple have five years from now? (See the time line depiction of this type of problem in figure 1.6.)

Figure 1.6
Time Line Representation of FVAD Problem

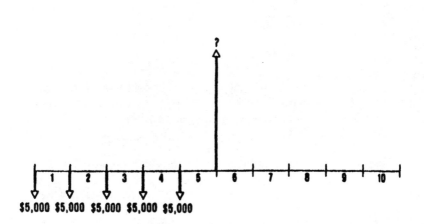

$5,000 $5,000 $5,000 $5,000 $5,000

This time line depicts a five-year annuity due. The problem is to determine the FVAD as of the end of the fifth year.

---

140.   Depress the following keys to reflect the known information: 5000, CHS (because, as was noted earlier, deposits that represent cash outflows are treated as negative numbers according to the cash flow sign convention), PMT, 8, i, 5, n, blue g, BEG (because the deposits are made at the start of each of the five years), and FV. The answer, the FVAD, $31,679.65, appears on the display. If the deposits had been made at the end of each of the five years, the keystrokes would be identical except for the substitution of END for BEG after blue g. The answer under this new assumption, the FVA, would be $29,333.00. You can produce this new solution simply by pressing blue g, END, and FV, rather than reentering all the information in the problem.

Using the HP-10B II

141.   If your calculator is the HP-10B II, clear the memory and set the machine to display two decimal places. In annuity and annuity due problems, you will be using a new key on the top row of the calculator, PMT, to reflect the fact that a series of deposits or payments is involved, rather than a single sum. Also, when solving problems involving a series of deposits or payments, you must *always* remember to instruct the calculator as to whether the deposits or payments will be made at the end of each period (FVA) or at the beginning (FVAD). This will be accomplished through the use of the shift key, and the BEG/END function printed on the MAR key near the top right-hand corner of the keyboard.

142.   To set the calculator to reflect when the payments occur in each period, press shift and BEG/END. The display will show either BEGIN or nothing. The latter means the calculator is set for end-of-period payments or deposits. If the setting is not the one you want for the problem at hand, press shift and BEG/END again. For now, set the calculator for beginning-of-period payments or deposits.

143.   To illustrate, assume that Henry and Etta deposit $5,000 today and again at the start of each of the next four years in their credit union account to accumulate funds for the lavish vacation they are planning in Bali. If the account is credited with 8 percent compound interest per year, how much will be in the account five years from now? (See the time line depiction of this problem in figure 1.6.)

144.   Press the following keys to reflect the known information: 5000, +/- (because, as noted earlier, deposits that represent cash outflows are treated as negative numbers), PMT, 5, N, 8, I/YR, and FV. The answer, the FVAD, $31,679.65, appears on the display. If the deposits had been made at the end of each of the five years, the keystrokes would be identical, except that you would set the calculator for end-of-period payments. The answer under this new assumption, the FVA, would be $29,333.00. You can produce this solution simply by pressing shift, BEG/END, and FV, rather than reentering all of the data in the problem.

Using the HP-17B II

145.   If your calculator is the HP-17B II, set it to display two decimal places and clear the TVM menu system's memory. In annuity and annuity due problems, you will be using a new menu key, the one for PMT, which is located between the PV and FV menu keys, to reflect the fact that a series of deposits or payments is involved, rather than a single sum. Also, when solving an annuity-type problem, you must *always* remember to instruct the calculator as to whether the payments or deposits will be made at the end of each period (FVA) or at the beginning (FVAD). This is accomplished by going to the TVM menu, pressing the OTHER menu key, and pressing the menu key for BEG or END, as appropriate. For now, set the calculator for BEG.

146.   To illustrate, assume that Jack and Jill deposit $5,000 today and again at the start of each of the next four years in their credit union savings account to accumulate funds for the purchase of a piece of land. If the account is credited with 8 percent compound interest per year, how much will be in the account five years from now? (See the time line depiction of this problem in figure 1.6).

147.   Press the following keys to reflect the known information: 5000, +/- (because, as noted earlier, deposits that represent cash outflows are treated as negative numbers), the PMT menu key, 8, the I%YR menu key, 5, and the N menu key. Now press the FV menu key and the answer, the FVAD, $31,679.65, appears on the screen. If the deposits had been made at the end of each year, rather than at the beginning, the answer, the FVA, would be 8 percent lower. You can produce the new solution without reentering all the data. Simply press the OTHER menu key, the END menu key, the EXIT key, and the FV menu key. The FVA is $29,333.00.

Using the BA-II Plus

148.   If you wish to use the BA-II Plus, clear the memory units and set the calculator to display two decimal places. In annuity and annuity due problems, you will be using a new key in the third row of the calculator keyboard, PMT, to reflect the fact that a series of deposits or payments is involved, rather than a single sum. Also, when solving a problem involving a series of

payments or deposits, you must *always* remember to instruct the calculator as to whether the payments or deposits will be made at the end of each period (FVA) or at the beginning (FVAD). This will be accomplished through the use of the 2nd key and the BGN function printed above the PMT key.

149.   To set the calculator to reflect when the payments occur in each period, press 2nd and BGN. The display will show either BGN or END. If the current setting is the one you want, press 2nd and QUIT. If the current setting is not the one you want, press 2nd, SET (which is printed above the ENTER key in the top row of the keyboard), 2nd, and QUIT. For now, set the machine for beginning-of-period payments.

150.   To illustrate, assume that a married couple deposits $5,000 today and at the start of each of the next four years in a savings account to accumulate funds for their young daughter's college education. If the account is credited with 8 percent compound interest per year, how much of a college fund will the couple have five years from now? (See the time line depiction of this problem in figure 1.6.)

151.   Depress the following keys to reflect the known information: 5000, +/- (because, as was noted earlier, deposits that represent cash outflows are treated as negative numbers), PMT, 5, N, 8, I/Y, CPT, and FV. The answer, the FVAD, $31,679.65, appears on the display. If the deposits had been made at the end of each of the five years, the keystrokes would be identical, except that you would set the calculator for end-of-period payments. The answer under this new assumption, the FVA, would be $29,333.00. You can produce this solution by pressing 2nd, BGN, 2nd, SET, 2nd, QUIT, CPT, and FV, rather than reentering all the information in the problem.

If Number of Compounding Periods Exceeds Number of Payments

152.   Sometimes, a problem will be encountered in which the number of periods during which compounding occurs exceeds the number of periods during which deposits are made. For example, assume that $500 is to be deposited at the end of each of the next six years in an account earning 8 percent compound annual interest. How much will be in the account at the end of ten years? (See figure 1.7.)

Figure 1.7
Time Line Representation of Problem Where Number of
Compounding Periods Exceeds Number of Deposits

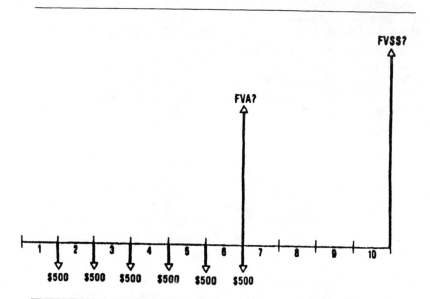

In this time line, level payments are made at the end of each of
six years. The future value of that annuity as of the end of the
sixth year is then left as a single sum to accumulate until the end
of the tenth year.

153.   The simplest way to solve a problem of this type is to
treat it as two separate problems and combine the results. The
first step is to compute the FVA; the second is to treat that value
as a single sum and compute its FVSS. You could use the FVA
formula to find the account's value of $3,667.96 at the end of six
years. Then use this amount in the FVSS formula to produce the
account value, namely, $4,990.22.

154.   Or, you can solve the problem on your calculator. Set it
for end-of-period payments and find the FVA of six $500
payments at 8 percent interest, which is $3,667.96. Enter this
amount as a PVSS with 8 percent as the interest rate and four as
the number of periods. Solve for FVSS, which is $4,990.22

Solving Sinking Fund Problems

155.   So far in this section, you have learned how to compute the future value of a series of payments or deposits when the number of payments, the rate of interest, and the size of each payment are known. Sometimes, however, the facts are different, and it is the size of the periodic payment that is the unknown of the four key elements. This is often called a sinking fund payment problem.

156.   For example, assume that a business wishes to accumulate $10,000,000 by the end of three years in order at that time to retire some of its outstanding mortgage bonds. The company plans to make three annual deposits, beginning today, into a sinking fund that will earn 9 percent compound interest. The question: how large must each of the deposits be in order to reach the target amount in three years?

157.   Although the answer can, of course, be found by rearranging the FVA or FVAD formula and solving for the amount of the deposit, the use of a financial calculator is much more efficient. Hence, only that method will be explained here.

158.   On the HP-12C, for example, press the following keys: 10000000, FV, 9, i, 3, n, blue g, BEG, and PMT. The answer, $2,798,667.50, is displayed on the screen (with a minus sign, in accordance with the cash flow sign convention).

159.   On the HP-10B II, set the calculator for beginning-of-period payments and press 10000000, FV, 9, I/YR, 3, N, and PMT. The answer, $2,798,667.50, is displayed (preceded by a minus sign, since these are outgoing payments).

160.   On the HP-17B II, set the machine for beginning-of-period payments and press 10000000, the FV menu key, 9, the I%YR menu key, 3, the N menu key, and the PMT menu key. The answer, $2,798,667.50, is displayed (with a minus sign, since these are outgoing payments).

161.   On the BA-II Plus, the same answer, again preceded by a minus sign, is found by setting the calculator for beginning-of-period payments and pressing 10000000, FV, 9, I/Y, 3, N, CPT, and PMT.[14]

162.   Variations from the foregoing sinking fund problem are problems in which the task is to compute the number of deposits that will be required or the interest rate that must be earned on the deposits in order to reach the target amount. For such purposes, a financial calculator is the most effective tool.

163.   Assume, for example, that you wish to accumulate $10,000 for a dream vacation on Kauai and that you can afford to save $1,200 per year, beginning a year from now, toward that objective. If your savings earn 10 percent compound annual interest, how long will you have to wait before you can buy your airline tickets?

164.   On the HP-12C, press 10000, FV, 10, i, 1200, CHS, PMT, blue g, END, and n to produce the answer, 7 years.

165.   On the HP-10B II, set the calculator for end-of-period payments and press 10000, FV, 10, I/YR, 1200, +/-, PMT, and N to produce the answer which, to four decimal places, is 6.3596 years.

166.   Or, set the HP-17B II for end-of-period payments and press 10000, the FV menu key, 10, the I%YR menu key, 1200, +/-, the PMT menu key, and the N menu key. The answer, to four decimal places, is 6.3596 years.

167.   On the BA-II Plus, set the calculator for end-of-period payments and press the following keys: 10000, FV, 10, I/Y, 1200, +/-, PMT, CPT, and N. The answer is 6.3596 years.[15]

168.   On the other hand, if you insist on waiting only five years before going to Kauai with your $10,000, what compound annual interest rate must you earn on your periodic deposits?

169.   On the HP-12C, press 10000, FV, 1200, CHS, PMT, 5, n, blue g, END, and i. The answer, hardly encouraging, will appear after a few seconds of running time as 25.7839 percent. The HP-10B, the HP-17B II, and the BA-II Plus provide no happier an answer.

170.   Set the HP-10B II for end-of-period payments and press 10000, FV, 1200, +/-, PMT, 5, N, and I/YR. The answer is an unlikely 25.7839 percent.

171.   With the HP-17B II set for end-of-period payments, press 10000, the FV menu key, 1200, +/-, the PMT menu key, 5, the N menu key, and the I%YR menu key. You'll have to find an investment that will earn 25.7839 percent.

172.   Or, set the BA-II Plus for end-of-period payments, press 10000, FV, 1200, +/-, PMT, 5, N, CPT, and I/Y to produce the answer after a few seconds, 25.7839 percent.

PRESENT VALUE OF AN ANNUITY OR ANNUITY DUE

173.   An earlier section of this chapter contained an explanation of how to calculate the present value of a *single* sum due or needed at some time in the future. This section expands on that case and deals with the question of how to compute the present value of a *series* of level future payments. This type of problem will be referred to as a present value of an annuity (PVA) problem if the payments are to be made at the end of each period or as a present value of an annuity due (PVAD) problem if they are to be made at the beginning of each period.

174.   To illustrate the type of problem that is the concern here, assume that an installment loan is to be repaid to you through six annual payments of $1,000 each, beginning one year from now. For how much would be willing to sell the promissory note today if you believe you can earn 8 percent compound annual interest on your money in some other investment outlet? What is the present value of this six-year annuity discounted at 8 percent?

Assumptions

175.   As was true in the preceding pages concerning the future value of a series of payments, it will be assumed here in the discussion of present value that each payment is made annually. This assumption will be dropped in the following chapter. In addition, it will be important to specify in each example whether the annuity payments are made at the end or at the beginning of each year. The difference in the answer can be substantial. For example, an eight-year, $1,000 annuity discounted at 6 percent has a PVA of $6,209.79, versus a PVAD of $6,582.38. (See figure 1.8.)

Figure 1.8
Time Line Representation of PVA and PVAD Problems

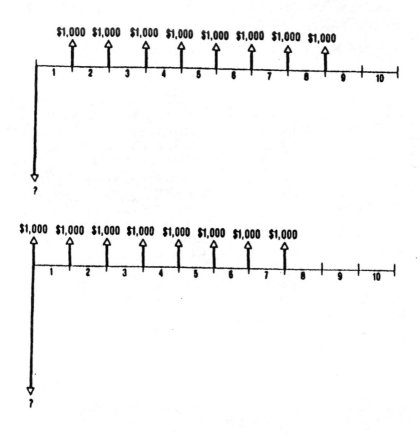

The upper time line depicts a case in which eight annual payments of $1,000 are to be made beginning in one year, and the problem is to compute the PVA. The lower time line depicts an eight-year annuity due, in which $1,000 payments are made at the start of each year, and the problem is to compute the PVAD.

Using a Time-Value Formula

176.   The basic formula for computing the present value of a single sum can also be used to compute the present value of an annuity or an annuity due. All that is needed is to calculate the PVSS for each annuity payment separately and total the results.

177.   For example, assume that as part of a divorce settlement, a father has been ordered to deposit a lump sum in trust sufficient to provide child support payments for his son. The child support payments are to be $5,000 per year for four years, beginning one year from today. If the amount placed in trust can be assumed to earn 7 percent compound annual interest, how much should the father place in the trust today?

178.   Through the formula described in the discussion of the present value of a single sum, the present value of each separate payment can be found. The amount to be deposited today would be equal to the combined present value of the four payments. Specifically, the present value of the first payment, to be made in one year, would be:

$$\text{PVSS} \quad = \quad \text{FVSS} \quad \left[\frac{1}{(1+i)^n} \right]$$

$$= \quad \$5,000 \quad \left[\frac{1}{(1.07)^1} \right]$$

$$= \quad \$5,000 \quad (.9346)$$

$$= \quad \$4,673.00$$

The present value of the second, third, and fourth payments would be as shown below:

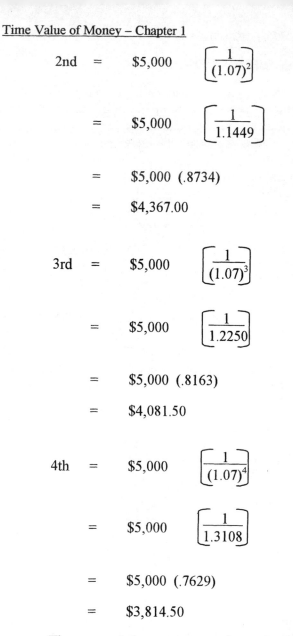

2nd $=$ $5,000 $\left[\dfrac{1}{(1.07)^2}\right]$

$=$ $5,000 $\left[\dfrac{1}{1.1449}\right]$

$=$ $5,000 (.8734)

$=$ $4,367.00

3rd $=$ $5,000 $\left[\dfrac{1}{(1.07)^3}\right]$

$=$ $5,000 $\left[\dfrac{1}{1.2250}\right]$

$=$ $5,000 (.8163)

$=$ $4,081.50

4th $=$ $5,000 $\left[\dfrac{1}{(1.07)^4}\right]$

$=$ $5,000 $\left[\dfrac{1}{1.3108}\right]$

$=$ $5,000 (.7629)

$=$ $3,814.50

The sum of these present values, the PVA would be ($4,673.00 + $4,367.00 + $4,081.50 + $3,814.50 =) $16,936.00. That amount, placed on deposit today at 7 percent compound annual interest, will be just enough (well, within $.07 of just enough) to provide four annual payments of $5,000 each, beginning in one year. To verify this, examine what would happen to the account each year.

Year	Beginning Balance	Interest Earnings	Amount Withdrawn	Ending Balance
1	$16,936.00	$1,185.52	$5,000.00	$13,121.52
2	$13,121.52	$ 918.51	$5,000.00	$ 9,040.03
3	$ 9,040.03	$ 632.80	$5,000.00	$ 4,672.83
4	$ 4,672.83	$ 327.10	$5,000.00	($ 0.07)

179.   If, on the other hand, the four annual payments were to be made beginning immediately, the PVAD would be as follows:

$$1st = PVSS = \$5,000 \left[\frac{1}{(1.07)^0} \right]$$

$$= \quad \$5,000 \ (1.0000) = \quad \$ 5,000.00$$

$$2nd = PVSS = \$5,000 \left[\frac{1}{(1.07)^1} \right]$$

$$= \quad \$5,000 \ (.9346) = \quad \$ 4,673.00$$

$$3rd = PVSS = \$5,000 \left[\frac{1}{(1.07)^2} \right]$$

$$= \quad \$5,000 \ (.8734) = \quad \$ 4,367.00$$

$$4th = PVSS = \$5,000 \left[\frac{1}{(1.07)^3} \right]$$

$$= \quad \$5,000 \ (.8163) = \quad \underline{\$ 4,081.50}$$

$$PVAD \qquad \qquad \$18,121.50$$

Why would a larger amount need to be deposited in trust if the payments are to begin immediately? The total interest earnings would be lower because each withdrawal to make the childsupport payments would occur a year earlier than under the end-of-year assumption.

180.   As an alternative to the foregoing approach of finding PVA or PVAD by summing the present value of each of the separate annuity payments, the same result can be achieved in one step by using the following, somewhat more complex formula.

$$PVA = \left[\frac{1 - \frac{1}{(1 + i)^n}}{i} \right] \text{(amount of one payment)}$$

Note that this formula should be used only for the case where the annuity payments are made at the end of each year.

181.   In the childsupport illustration, then,

$$PVA = \left[\frac{1 - \frac{1}{(1.07)^4}}{.07} \right] (\$5,000)$$

$$= \left[\frac{1 - \frac{1}{1.3108}}{.07} \right] (\$5,000)$$

Note that this formula should be used only for the case where the annuity payments are made at the end of each year.

$$= \left[\frac{.2371}{.07} \right] (\$5,000)$$

$$= (3.3871) \ (\$5,000)$$

$$= \$16,935.50$$

182.   For cases in which the payments are to be made at the beginning of each year, the same formula may be used, but with one important modification. To reflect the fact that each payment will earn one fewer year of interest before it is distributed, it is necessary to multiply the result of the preceding formula by $(1+i)$. That is, if the payments are made at the beginning of each year, the formula becomes:

$$PVAD = (1+i) \left[\frac{1 - \frac{1}{(1+i)^n}}{i} \right] \quad \text{(amount of one payment)}$$

$$= (1.07) \left[\frac{1 - \frac{1}{(1.07)^4}}{.07} \right] \quad (\$5,000)$$

$$= (1.07) \left[\frac{.2371}{.07} \right] \quad (\$5,000)$$

$$= (1.07) \ (\$16,935.50)$$

$$= \$18,120.99$$

As was done in converting from FVA to FVAD, then, the way to compute PVAD is to compute PVA and then multiply the result by $(1 + i)$.

Using a Financial Calculator To Compute PVA and PVAD

183.   Use of an electronic calculator with finance functions greatly eases the task of calculating the present value of an annuity or of an annuity due. The calculator is faster, is less likely to produce mistakes, and allows for the selection of many values for n and i without having to work manually through the recalculation process.

Using the HP-12C

184.   Assume that a woman receives $15,000 each year from a trust. She is interested in obtaining a cash sum with which to buy a fancy new sports car. Her cousin has offered to buy from

her now the present value of the next four annuity payments (the first of which will be made one year from now) discounted at 8 percent compound annual interest. How much will the woman receive if she accepts the offer?

185.   If you are using the HP-12C, clear the memory units and set the calculator to display two decimal places. Then depress the following keys to enter the known information: 15000, PMT (because the problem involves a series of payments, rather than a single sum), 8, i, 4, n, blue g, and END (because the payments will be made at the end of each year). The calculator is now programmed to compute the PVA. Depress the PV key and the answer, $49,681.90, is displayed on the screen (as a negative, because it is a present value).

186.   If the facts of the problem were revised so that the four annual payments from the trust were to begin immediately, the procedure for solving it would be identical, except that the BEG key would be pressed instead of the END key. You can solve it now by pressing blue g, BEG, and PV. The answer, the PVAD, is $53,656.45.

Using the HP-10B II

187.   Under the terms of a structured settlement in a lawsuit Donna just won, she is to receive $25,000 per year at the end of each of the next 15 years. She believes that, if she had a lump sum of money today, she could put it to work to earn 7½ percent compound annual interest. If so, what lump sum today would be the equivalent of the payments Donna is scheduled to receive?

188.   Clear the memory of the HP-10B II and set it to display two decimal places. Also, set it for end-of-period payments since the first one won't occur until a year from now. Then press the following keys to enter the known information: 25000, PMT (because the problem involves a series of payments, rather than a single sum), 15, N, 7.5, and I/YR. The calculator is now programmed to find the PVA. Press PV, and the answer, $220,677.99, will be displayed (as a negative, because it is a present value). If the facts of the problem were changed so that the annual payments were to begin immediately, their present value, the PVAD, would be higher by one year's interest. Press shift, BEG/END, and PV to find the answer, $237,228.84. Note that this amount is 7½ percent greater than $220,677.99.

Using the HP-17B II

189.   Assume that you have just won the lottery and are scheduled to receive $15,000 at the end of each of the next ten years. If the going rate of interest is 7 percent, how much have you won in present-value terms?

190.   Clear the TVM menu system and set the calculator for end-of-period payments. Then enter the known information as follows: 10, the N menu key, 15000, the PMT menu key (because the problem involves a series of payments, rather than a single sum), 7, and the I%YR menu key. Now press the PV menu key, and the answer, $105,353.72, will be displayed (as a negative, because it is a present value).

191.   If the lottery payments were to begin immediately, they would have a higher present value. Reset the calculator for beginning-of-period payments by pressing the Other menu key, the BEG menu key, and EXIT. Then press PV again to find the PVAD, $112,728.48. Note that this figure exceeds the PVA of $105,353.72 by 7 percent, the amount of one year's interest.

Using the BA-II Plus

192.   Assume that several years ago, the owner of a small business borrowed $10,000 from a relative and agreed to repay the loan in ten equal annual installments of $1,500 each.   Six payments remain to be made, the first of which is due in one year. The business owner now would like to pay off the remainder of the debt.   What sum should the business owner propose to the lender as a payoff figure if money is presently worth 7 percent?

193.   If you are using the BA-II Plus, clear the memory units, set the calculator to display two decimal places, and set it for end-of-period payments (because the payments will be made at the end of each year).   Then depress the following keys to enter the known information: 1500, PMT (because the problem involves a series of payments, rather than a single sum), 6, N, 7, I/Y, and CPT. The calculator is now programmed to compute the PVA. Depress the PV key, and the answer, $7,149.81, is displayed on the screen (as a negative, because it is a present value).

194.   If the facts of the problem were revised so that the remaining six annual payments were to be made beginning immediately, the procedure for solving it would be identical, except that the calculator should be set for beginning-of-period payments. You can solve it now by pressing 2nd, BGN, 2nd, SET, 2nd, QUIT, CPT, and PV. The answer, the PVAD, is $7,650.30, which is 7 percent, or one year's interest, greater than the PVA.

If Number of Discounting Periods Exceeds Number of Payments

195.   Sometimes, a problem will be encountered in which the number of periods during which discounting is to occur exceeds the number of periods during which annuity payments are to be made. For example, what is the present value at a 7 percent compound annual interest rate of an income stream consisting of five annual payments of $2,000 each, the first of which will be made three years from now? (See the time line depiction of this type of problem in figure 1.9.)

Figure 1.9

Time Line Depiction of PVA or PVAD Problems Where Number of Discounting Periods Exceeds Payment Periods

---

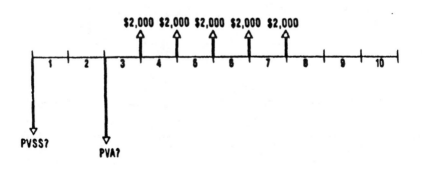

This time line depicts a case in which five annual payments of $2,000 each are to be made, beginning in three years. The problem, which is to determine the present value of the income stream, can be divided into two parts. First, determine the present value of the annuity as of the start of the annuity period, which is the beginning of year *three*. (Note: It is not the beginning of year four, even though that is when the first payment will be made.) Then, compute the present value of that single sum as of today, two (not three) years earlier.

196.   The simplest way to solve a problem of this type, called a deferred annuity problem, is to treat it as two separate problems and combine the results. The first step is to compute the PVA; the second is to treat that value as a single sum and compute its PVSS.

197.   If you use the PVA formula, you will find a value of $8,200.39 at the start of year three. Then use the PVSS formula to discount this amount for two more years. The answer is $7,162.54.

198.   If you are using the HP-12C, HP-10B II, HP-17B II, or BA-II Plus calculator for this type of problem, compute the PVA in the usual manner. However, be sure to then fully clear the calculator's memory units before you proceed to the second step of the problem. Then enter the PVA you just calculated as a future value and compute its present value in the normal way.

199.   Note that in this solution, a PVA was calculated and then discounted as a single sum for two additional years. The same result can be achieved if the problem is viewed as entailing the calculation of a PVAD and then discounting that single sum for three additional years. (Reexamine figure 1.9 to verify that a five-year PVA discounted for an additional two years is identical to a five-year PVAD discounted for an additional three years.)

Solving Debt Service/Capital Sum Liquidation Problems

200.   Thus far, you have seen how to compute the present value of a stream of equal payments when the number of payments, the rate of interest, and the size of each payment are

known. Sometimes, however, it is the size of the periodic payment that is the unknown of the four key elements. A frequently encountered problem of this type is that of determining the amount of money necessary to liquidate a debt through periodic loan repayments. A similar problem is to determine how large a periodic withdrawal from a sum of capital can be in order to liquidate that sum over a given number of years.

201.   In installment loans such as those used to finance the purchase of a house or automobile, each level periodic payment, called the debt service, consists of some repayment of the principal and some payment of interest on the remaining unpaid principal. Given the initial size of the loan, the interest rate, and the number of payments to be made, the problem is to compute the size of each required payment.[16]

202.   For example, assume that a real estate mortgage for a certain amount and with a known interest rate is to be repaid in a certain number of equal annual installments, the first to be made in one year. The question: How large must each annual installment payment be? Although the answer can be found by rearranging the PVA formula and solving for the amount of the payment, that procedure is complex and unwieldy in comparison with using a financial calculator. Hence, only the calculator method will be explained here.

203.   To illustrate the procedure, assume that in a negligence case, a jury has awarded $125,000 to be used to support an injured child until the child reaches age 21, eleven years from now. How much will this capital sum and interest earnings thereon provide for the child per year if the fund earns 8 percent compound interest?

204.   On the HP-12C, depress the following keys: 125000, CHS, PV, 8, i, 11, n, blue g, BEG (or END, depending on when the first withdrawal will be made), and PMT. The payment under the beginning-of-year assumption is $16,212.54. Under the end-of-year assumption, it is $17,509.54.

205.   On the HP-10B II, set the machine for beginning-of-period or end-of-period payments, depending on when the eleven payments will be made.   Then press 125000, +/-, PV, 8, I/YR, 11, N, and PMT.   The payment will be $16,212.54 under the beginning-of-year assumption or $17,509.54 under the end-of-year assumption.

206.   Or, on the HP-17B II, set the machine for beginning-of-period payments.   Press 125000, +/-, the PV menu key, 8, the I%YR menu key, 11, the N menu key, and the PMT menu key. The answer is $16,212.54.   Now see what the payment would be if an end-of-period assumption is used.   Press the OTHER menu key, the END menu key, the EXIT key, and the PMT menu key. The answer is $17,509.54.

207.   On the BA-II Plus, the answers are found by setting the calculator for beginning- or end-of-period payments and pressing 125000, +/-, PV, 8, I/Y, 11, N, CPT, and PMT.   The payment will be $16,212.54 if made at the start of each or $17,509.54 if made at the end of each year.

208.   Debt-service problems are always solved under an end-of-period assumption.   Capital sum liquidation problems may call for the use of either an end-of-period or beginning-of-period assumption.

209.   Variations from the most common debt service and capital sum liquidation problems are problems in which the task is to compute n, the number of installment payments that will be required or possible, or i, the interest rate being charged or needed.

210.   Assume, for example, that a company plans to borrow $200,000 to expand its fleet of delivery vehicles.   If the financial officer believes the company can afford to make loan repayments of $55,000 per year, beginning a year from now, and if the lending institution is charging an interest rate of 10.5 percent, how long will it take to repay the loan?

211.   On the HP-12C, press 200000, CHS, PV, 55000, PMT, blue g, END, 10.5, i, and n. The answer is five years.

212.   Or, set the HP-10B II for end-of-period payments and four decimal places. Then press 200000, +/-, PV, 55000, PMT, 10.5, I/YR, and N. The answer is 4.8172 years.

213.   Or, set the HP-17B II for end-of-period payments and four decimal places. Press 200000, +/-, the PV menu key, 55000, the PMT menu key, 10.5, and the I%YR menu key. Then press the N menu key to obtain the answer, 4.8172 years.

214.   Or, on the BA-II Plus, press the following keys after setting the calculator for end-of-period payments and four decimal places: 200000, +/-, PV, 55000, PMT, 10.5, I/Y, CPT, and N. The answer is 4.8172 years.[17]

215.   On the other hand, if the financial officer believes the company must have the loan repaid in four years, what interest rate must he or she obtain from the lending institution to accomplish this objective?

216.   On the HP-12C, press 200000, CHS, PV, 55000, PMT, 4, n, blue g, END, and i. The answer, an unlikely 3.9245 percent, will eventually appear on the screen.

217.   Even if the borrower and lender use the HP-10B II, the HP-17B II, or the BA-II Plus, they are unlikely to reach agreement on an acceptable interest rate. Set the calculator for end-of-period payments.

218.   Then on the HP-10B II, press 200000, +/-, PV, 55000, PMT, 4, N, and I/YR.

219.   Or, on the HP-17B II press 200000, +/-, the PV menu key, 55000, the PMT menu key, 4, the N menu key, and the I%YR menu key.

220.   Or, on the BA-II Plus press 200000, +/-, PV, 55000, PMT, 4, N, CPT, and I/Y. After a brief delay, the 3.9245 percent rate is displayed.

Creating an Amortization Schedule

221.   Another useful calculation in connection with debt service problems is to generate an amortization schedule. In any installment loan, a portion of each payment is used to pay interest, and the rest is applied to reduce the principal of the loan. Over the term of the loan, the interest portion of the payment falls, and the principal portion rises. The amortization schedule enables you to see, year by year, how much is being applied toward each.

222.   To illustrate, assume that a $1,000 loan with a compound annual interest rate of 11 percent is to be repaid in four equal annual installments, beginning in one year. The amount of each payment is $322.33. How much of each year's payment will be applied to interest and how much to principal?[18]

223.   If you are preparing the amortization schedule manually, you should set up a worksheet with column headings as shown in the following table.

TABLE 1.3
Sample Loan Amortization Schedule

	(1)	(2)	(3)	(4)	(5)
Year	Unpaid Balance, Beg. of Year	Payment, End of Year	Interest Payment 11% x (1)	Principal Payment (2)-(3)	Unpaid Balance End of Year (1)-(4)
1	$1,000.00	$322.33	$110.00	$212.33	$787.67
2	787.67	322.33	86.64	235.69	551.98
3	551.98	322.33	60.72	261.61	290.37
4	290.37	322.33	31.94	290.39	(.02)

224.   After inserting the initial loan amount and the first year's payment, calculate the first year's interest by multiplying the 11 percent interest rate by the loan amount. This produces the figure for column (3). The balance of the payment, shown in column (4), is applied to the principal and is subtracted from the initial loan amount to produce the unpaid balance at the end of the first year, as shown in column (5). This amount is also the unpaid balance at the beginning of the second year, as shown in column (1). Again, 11 percent of this amount is the second year's interest in column (3), the remainder of the payment goes on principal in column (4), and so on through the end of the fourth and final year of the loan.

Using the HP-12C

225.   If you are using the HP-12C to create an amortization schedule, note that the n key also contains a yellow AMORT (amortization) function. Note also the x ≥ key in the second row from the bottom of the keyboard. Both of these will be used to solve the problem.

226.   First, enter the basic data about the problem in this illustration. Press 11, i, blue g, END, 4, n, 1000, PV, 322.33, CHS, and PMT. Now press 1 (because one payment will be made per year), yellow f, and AMORT. The amount displayed,

$110.00, is the first year's interest. Next press the x ≥ key to see the principal payment, $212.33. Then press RCL (the Recall key in the bottom row of the keyboard) and PV to show the unpaid balance at the end of year one, $787.67. Repeat the sequence as shown below to see the amounts in the following years.

Year	Keystroke	Interest	Keystroke	Principal	Keystroke	Unpaid Balance
2	1, yellow f, AMORT	$86.64	x ≥	$235.69	RCL, PV	$551.98
3	1, yellow f, AMORT	$60.72	x ≥	$261.61	RCL, PV	$290.37
4	1, yellow f AMORT	$31.94	x ≥	$290.39	RCL, PV	($ .02)

The total interest paid during the four years is, thus, ($110.00 + $86.64 + $60.72 + $31.94 =) $289.30. The principal repaid, of course, totals (except for $.02 due to rounding) $1,000.

Using the HP-10B II

227.   In order to create an amortization schedule using the HP-10B II calculator, set the machine for end-of-period payments and two decimal places. Then enter the basic data about the problem in this illustration by pressing 4, N, 11, I/YR, 1000, PV, 322.33, +/-, and PMT. Next press 1 and the INPUT key near the top left-hand corner of the keyboard to tell the machine that you want to see the amortization values for the first payment. Then press shift and AMORT, which is printed on the FV key. The display will show PER 1-1. Now press = to show the amount of the first payment that was applied against principal, $212.33. Press = again to see the first year's interest, $110.00, and press = again to show the loan balance at the end of the first year, $787.67. Now press 2, INPUT, shift, AMORT, = (to show the second year's principal payment, $235.69), = again (to show the second year's interest, $86.64), and press = again (to show the loan balance after two years, $551.98), 3, INPUT, shift, AMORT, = (to show the third year's principal payment, $261.61), = (to show the third year's interest, $60.72), and press = again (to show the loan balance after three payments have been made, $290.37), 4, INPUT, shift, AMORT, = (to show that

$290.39 of the fourth payment went on principal), = (to show the fourth year's interest , $31.94), and = (to show the unpaid loan balance at the end of year four of zero, except for a difference of $.02 due to rounding).

228.   If you wish to see a summary of the four years' results, press 1, INPUT, 4, shift, AMORT, = (to show the total principal paid, which is, of course, $1,000 (plus $.02 due to rounding), and = (to show the total interest paid of $289.30).

Using the HP-17B II

229.   In order to create an amortization schedule for this problem on the HP-17B II, set the machine to display 2 decimal places. Also set it for end-of-period payments. Then enter the basic data about the problem in this illustration: 4, the N menu key, 11, the I%YR menu key, 1000, the PV menu key, 322.33, +/-, and the PMT menu key. Now press the OTHER menu key and the AMRT menu key. Next, press 1 and the #P menu key. Now you are ready to see the year-by-year results. Press the INT menu key to see that $110 of interest is paid in the first year, the PRIN menu key to see that $212.33 of principal is paid in the first year, and the BAL menu key to see that the unpaid balance at the end of the first year is $787.67. Now press the NEXT menu key, the INT menu key to see that $86.64 of interest is paid in the second year, the PRIN menu key to see that $235.69 of principal is paid in the second year, and the BAL menu key to see the unpaid balance, $551.98, at the end of the second year. Press the NEXT menu key followed by the INT menu keys for the third year's interest, $60.72; the PRIN menu key for the third year's principal payment, $261.61; and the BAL menu key to show that $290.37 is owed at the end of the third year. Complete the schedule by pressing the NEXT menu key, the INT menu key ($31.94), the PRIN menu key ($290.39), and the BAL menu key (–$.02).

230.   If you wish to see a summary of the results for the four years, press EXIT, the AMORT menu key, 4, #P, the INT menu key to see that $289.30 is paid in interest. Press the PRIN and BAL menu keys to show that the loan is repaid in full. Press EXIT twice to return to the TVM menu.

Using the BA-II Plus

231.   The procedure for creating an amortization schedule on the BA-II Plus calculator requires that you leave the machine's standard-calculator mode that has been used throughout this chapter and use its prompted-worksheet mode. First, however, clear the memory units and set the calculator for end-of-period payments and two decimal places. Then enter the basic data about the problem in this illustration by pressing the following keys: 1000, PV, 11, I/Y, 4, N, 322.33, +/-, and PMT.

232.   Then to create the schedule, you will be using the Amort (amortization) function on the PV key, the ENTER key on the top row of the keyboard, and the down-arrow key next to the ON/OFF key. Press the following keys:

2nd, Amort   (to access the amortization prompted-worksheet mode)

1, ENTER, ↓, 1,   (to show the unpaid loan balance after the
ENTER, ↓   first payment, $787.67)

↓   (to show how much of the first payment was applied to principal, $212.33)

↓   (to show how much of the first payment was applied to interest, $110.00)

↓, ↓, 2,   (to show the unpaid loan balance after the
ENTER, ↓   second payment, $551.98)

↓   (to show the cumulative total applied to principal to this point, $448.02)

↓   (to show the cumulative total applied to interest to this point, $196.64)

↓, ↓, 3,   (to show the unpaid loan balance after the
ENTER, ↓   third payment, $290.37)

↓   (to show the cumulative total applied to principal to this point, $709.63)

↓	(to show the cumulative total applied to interest to this point, $257.36)
↓, ↓, 4, ENTER, ↓	(to show an unpaid loan balance of approximately zero after the fourth and final payment)
↓	(to show the approximate cumulative total applied to principal by the end of the loan period, $1,000)
↓	(to show the approximate cumulative total applied as interest by the end of the loan period, $289.30)

233.   When you have completed your review of the amortization schedule, clear this prompted worksheet and all the memory registers and return to the standard-calculator mode by pressing 2nd, Amort, 2nd, CLR Work, 2nd, Quit, 2nd, and CLR TVM.

PROBLEMS INVOLVING BOTH SINGLE SUMS AND ANNUITIES

234.   Earlier in this chapter, we noted that, though most time-value-of-money problems involve only four variables, sometimes they involve five variables, of which four are known, and the task is to solve for the fifth. For example, a problem might involve an initial deposit of $1,000 into a savings account, annual deposits of $300 at the end of years one, two, and three, and compound annual interest earnings of 7 percent on all the deposits. The task might be to compute the account balance at the end of the third year.

235.   Problems such as these are simply combinations of the types of problems you have already learned to solve. Simply divide the problem into its component parts, solve each component separately, and combine the solutions together.

236.   To illustrate, the preceding problem is made up of an FVSS problem ($1,000 for three years at 7 percent) and an FVA problem ($300 at the end of each year for three years at 7 percent). If you use the appropriate formulas, you will find the

FVA to be $964.47 and the FVSS to be $1,225.04. Therefore, the account balance will be $2,189.51.

237.   To revise part of this problem a bit, what if the objective is to have $2,500 in the account at the end of the third year? What initial deposit will be needed, together with the three annual deposits, to reach this goal? This problem involves calculating the FVA of the three $300 deposits, subtracting it from the $2,500 future goal, and computing the PVSS of the balance. $2,500.00 – $964.47 = $1,535.53. This amount, discounted for three years at 7%, has a PV of $1,253.45.

238.   If you are using a financial calculator, the task is somewhat simpler. In the first problem, enter $1,000 as the negative PV, $300 as the negative end-of-period payment, 3 as the n or N, and 7 as the interest rate. Then solve for FV, which will be $2,189.51. In the second problem, enter $2,500 as the FV, $300 as the negative end-of-period payment, 3 as the n or N, and 7 as the interest rate. Then solve for PV, which will be a negative $1,253.45.

239.   A frequent situation calling for the calculation of a fifth variable on the basis of four known variables is the computation of a bond's yield to maturity. For example, what is the yield to maturity of a $1,000 face amount bond, currently selling for $920, that will mature in six years and, in the meantime, will pay $80 of interest at the end of each year?[19] Enter $1,000 as the FV, $920 as the negative PV, 6 as the n or N, and $80 as the end-of-period payment. Then solve for the interest rate, which is 9.83%.

NOTES

1.   Problems of this type are discussed briefly at the end of this chapter.

2.   The descriptions provided for the solution of problems using the HP-12C, the HP-10B II, the HP-17B II, and the BA-II Plus are for educational purposes only and should not be construed as an endorsement of them by either the author or the publisher. None of these is the most sophisticated calculator marketed by the two manufacturers. However, these four calculators are relatively inexpensive and can be used to solve any type of time-value-of-money problem described in this book.

3.   Several keys on the HP-12C calculator perform more than one function. This is accomplished by means of the yellow f key and blue g key on the bottom row of the keyboard. Pressing yellow f and a key causes the key to perform the function printed in yellow above that key. Pressing blue g and a key causes the key to perform the function printed in blue on the lower edge of that key. For example, press the 9, ENTER, 2, and y^x keys. The number 81, which is 9 squared, appears on the display. Now press CLX, 9, ENTER, blue g, and the same y^x key. The number 3, which is the square root of 9, appears on the display. Pressing the blue g key switched the function to be performed by the y^x key from raising the number to a power (y^x), in this case squaring it, to finding its square root ($\sqrt{x}$).

4.   For your convenience, Appendix A lists the keystrokes to be used in solving the most common types of time-value-of-money problems on the HP-12C.

5.   Several keys on the HP-10B II calculator perform more than one function. This is accomplished by the orange shift key. Pressing this key and another key causes the latter key to perform the function printed in color below it. For example, press the orange shift key and the ON key, which has OFF printed below it, to turn the calculator off. Turn it on again, then press 9, shift, x (which has y^x printed below it), 4, and =. The

number 6,561 appears on the display screen. You have just raised the number 9 to the fourth power (9 x 9 x 9 x 9) by means of the y^x function that is activated by the shifted x key. (You will note that the calculator also has a mauve key above the orange one. The mauve key is not used in solving TVM problems, so it is ignored in this book.)

6.   For your convenience, Appendix B lists the keystrokes to be used in performing various housekeeping functions and in solving the most common types of time-value-of-money problems on the HP-10B II.

7.   Several keys on the HP-17B II calculator perform more than one function. This is accomplished by the colored shift key, ■. Pressing this key and another key causes the latter key to perform the function printed in color above it. For example, press the shift key and the CLR key, which has OFF printed above it, to turn the calculator off. Turn it on again, then press 9, shift, x (which has y^x printed above it), 4, and =. The number 6,561 appears on the display screen. You have just raised the number 9 to the fourth power (9 x 9 x 9 x 9) by means of the y^x function that is activated by the shifted x key.

8.   For your convenience, Appendix C lists the keystrokes to be used in performing various housekeeping functions and in solving the most common types of time-value-of-money problems on the HP-17B II.

9.   Several keys on the BA-II Plus keyboard perform two separate functions. The first function is that printed on the key. The second is that printed directly above it. This latter function is performed by pressing the grey key marked 2nd in the upper left-hand corner of the keyboard, followed by the key in question.

10.   For your convenience, Appendix D lists the keystrokes to be used in solving the most common types of time-value-of-money problems on the BA-II Plus.

11.   The rule of 72 can be used for purposes of discounting, as well as for compounding, as will be explained later. In that case, the result of dividing the number 72 by the interest rate is the approximate number of periods it will take to produce a present value equal to one-half the original sum.

12.   Specifically, the formula is as follows:

$$n = \frac{\log\left[\dfrac{FVSS}{PVSS}\right]}{\log\ (1+i)}$$

13.   In some fields, such as insurance, the terms "annuity" and "annuity due" are used to refer to a series of payments, the value of which includes both compound interest *and mortality* factors. Such annuities are often referred to as *life* annuities or *life* annuities due.

14.   If the sinking fund payments were to be made at the end of each of the three years, the method of solving the problem would be slightly different. On the HP-12C, press END after blue g, rather than BEG. On the HP-10B II, the HP-17B II, or the BA-II Plus, set the machine for end-of-period payments and recompute the payment. The precise answer is $3,050,547.57. The larger deposits are necessitated, of course, by the fact that each deposit will earn interest for one year less under the end-of-year assumption.

15.   Technically, this answer assumes that in the seventh year, a fraction of a year's interest is earned, and a fraction of one annual deposit is also added to the account. As was explained earlier, the HP-12C is less precise than the HP-10B II, the HP-17B II, or the BA-II plus in solving for n.

16.   In reality, most installment loans call for monthly payments. In this chapter, however, it will be assumed that the periodic loan payments are made annually. The method for

computing monthly payments will be explained in the next chapter.

17.   As was explained earlier, the HP-12C is less precise than the HP-10B II, the HP-17B II, or the BA-II Plus in solving for n. Also, technically, the precise answer of 4.8172 years assumes that in the final year, a fraction of a year's interest is paid, as well as a fraction of a full year's loan payment.

18.   The procedure for creating an amortization schedule where the loan is repaid through monthly installment payments is the same as described in this section, except that: (a) the figure used as the periodic payment should be the monthly payment; (b) the figure used as the interest rate should be the annual rate divided by 12; and (c) the number used as the n should be the total number of monthly payments to be made. See the discussion of simple annuities in the following chapter.

19.   The solution when a bond pays interest semiannually, as is the usual case, will be explained in the next chapter.

PROBLEMS

1.   A real estate appraiser has advised you that the value of homes in your neighborhood has been rising at a compound annual rate of about 6 percent in recent years. On the basis of this information, what is the value today of the home you bought seven years ago for $119,500?

2.   According to the rule of 72, approximately how long will it take for a sum of money to double in value if it earns a compound annual interest rate of 4 percent?

3.   Although you have made no deposits or withdrawals from your emergency fund savings account at the bank, the account balance has risen during the past three years from $15,000 to $17,613.62.

(a)   What has been the compound annual interest rate that the bank has been crediting to your account?

(b)   At that rate, how many more years will be needed until your account balance reaches $20,000?

4.   There is an attractive piece of undeveloped land that you are considering purchasing. You think that in five years it will sell for $30,000. What would you pay for it today if you want to earn a compound annual rate of return of 12 percent on your investment?

5.   Your personal net worth has risen in the past four years from $110,000 to $260,000 due to your shrewd investing. What has been the compound annual rate of growth of your net worth during this period?

6.   You hope to accumulate $45,000 as a down payment on a vacation home in the near future.

(a)   If you can set aside $38,000 now in an account that will be credited with 8 percent compound annual interest, how long will it take until you have the needed down payment?

(b)   What if you can get 9 percent per year on your money?

7.   You have decided that, beginning one year from now, you are going to deposit your $1,200 annual dividend check in a savings account at the credit union to build up a retirement fund. The account will be credited with 6 percent compound annual interest.

        (a)   If you plan to retire 18 years from now, how much will be in the account at that time?

        (b)   If you should decide to retire three years earlier than that, how much will be in the account?

8.   The round-the-world-trip you and your spouse intend on taking on your 25th wedding anniversary, six years from now, will cost $22,000.

        (a)   How much should you set aside each year, beginning today, to reach that objective if you can earn 9 percent compound annual interest on your money?

        (b)   How will the size of the annual deposit be affected if you can earn only 8 percent compound annual interest?

9.   You have just started a program of depositing $2,000 at the beginning of each year in an education fund account for your newborn son. How much will be in the account:

        (a)   After 11 years if it earns 8.5 percent compound annual interest

        (b)   After 13 years if it earns 8.5 percent compound annual interest

        (c)   After 18 years if it earns 7.5 percent compound annual interest and you discontinue making deposits after the fifth deposit

10.   A company leases an office building you own for $25,000 each year. The next rental payment is due in one year.

        (a)   For what lump-sum amount would you sell the next three payments today if you could invest the proceeds at a 12.5 percent compound annual rate of return?

(b)   For what amount would you sell them if the next rental payment is due later today?

11.   Which would you prefer to have: $10,000 today in a lump sum or $1,000 per year for 13 years, beginning one year from now, if interest rates are:

(a)   4 percent

(b)   6 percent

12.   A bank is willing to lend you $15,000 to make some home improvements. The loan is to be repaid in five equal annual installments, beginning one year from now. If the interest rate on the loan is 10 percent:

(a)   What will be the size of the annual payment?

(b)   How much of the second payment will be interest?

(c)   How much of the final payment will be principal?

13.   The account in which you deposited your inheritance has a present balance of $48,000. If the account is credited with 13 percent compound annual interest, and if you plan to withdraw from it $7,500 per year, beginning one year from now, how long will it be before the balance is zero?

14.   Suppose that a bank will lend you $10,000 if you agree to repay $4,199.31 at the end of each of the next three years. What compound annual interest rate is the bank charging you?

15.   If you deposit $1,100 in your bank account today and add deposits of $600 to it at the end of each of the next nine years, and if all your deposits earn 6 percent compound annual interest, how much will be in your account immediately after you make the last deposit?

SOLUTIONS

Editor's Note: Solutions to most of the problems at the end of this and the next two chapters have been calculated with the answers rounded to two decimal places for dollar values and four decimal places for interest rate values (here abbreviated as i) and values for the number of periods (here abbreviated as n). If you use formulas to solve these problems, your solutions may vary slightly from those presented due to rounding differences.

1.   The house should be worth about $179,700 today. On a financial calculator, $119,500 compounded at 6 percent for 7 years produces FV = $179,683.82.

2.   At a 4 percent compound annual interest rate, according to the rule of 72, it will take about 18 years for a sum of money to double in value because $72 \div 4 = 18$. A more precise answer, found by means of a financial calculator, is n = 17.6730.

3.   (a)   Your account has been credited with 5.5 percent compound annual interest. On a financial calculator with $15,000 as the PV, $17,613.62 as the FV, and 3 as the n, i = 5.5000 percent.

     (b)   Your account balance will reach $20,000 in a little more than 2 years. On the HP-10B II, the HP-17B II, or the BA-II Plus financial calculator, with $20,000 as the FV, $17,613.62 as the PV, and 5.5 as the i, you can find that the precise n = 2.3731 (rounded to 3 on the HP-12C calculator).

4.   You should be willing to pay about $17,000 for the property today. With a financial calculator, $30,000 discounted at 12 percent for 5 years produces PV = $17,022.81.

5.   Your net worth has grown at a compound annual rate of almost 24 percent. Through the use of a financial calculator, with $110,000 as the PV, $260,000 as the FV, and 4 as the n, you could calculate the precise i of 23.9924 percent.

6. (a) It will take a little over 2 years to accumulate the down payment. With a financial calculator, and with $45,000 as the FV, $38,000 as the PV, and 8 as the i, you could find that the precise n = 2.1969. (Note, however, that the HP-12C produces an imprecise n = 3.)

(b) With a higher rate, the waiting period is shortened to just under 2 years. If you use a financial calculator, enter 9 as i, and you will see that n = 1.9619.

7. (a) If you use a financial calculator, with $1,200 as the end-of-period PMT, 18 as n, and 6 as i, FVA = $37,086.78.

(b) At the end of 15 years, the account balance will be about $27,931. If you use a financial calculator, insert 15 as the n to find FVA = $27,931.16.

8. (a) You should set aside approximately $2,683 now and at the beginning of each of the next 5 years in order to reach the target amount. The target amount, $22,000, is the FV, 6 is the n, and 9 is the i. The beginning-of-year PMT = $2,682.78.

(b) If only 8 percent compound annual interest is earned, the size of the needed annual deposit rises to about $2,777. On the calculator, enter 8 as the i, and the beginning-of-year PMT = $2,776.79.

9. (a) After 11 years at 8.5 percent, there will be approximately $37,099 in the account. On the calculator, enter 11 as n, 8.5 as i, and $2,000 as the beginning-of-year PMT. FVAD = $37,098.50.

(b) After 13 years at 8.5 percent, there will be about $48,198 in the account. On the financial calculator, replacing 11 with 13 as n produces FVAD = $48,197.73.

(c) At the end of 5 years, there will be about $12,488 in the account. If you use a financial calculator, replace n with 5 and i with 7.5. $12,488.04 will be in the account at the end of 5 years. Clear the machine and reenter this as the PV, with 7.5 as the i and 13 as the n. FV = $31,974.54.

10.   (a)   You would be willing to sell the next three payments for about $59,533 today. On a financial calculator with $25,000 as the end-of-year PMT, 3 as the n, and 12.5 as the i, PVA = $59,533.61.

    (b)   In this case, the selling price would be higher, about $66,975. Change from the end-of-period mode to the beginning-of-period mode. The present value of the three beginning-of-year PMTs is $66,975.31.

11.   (a) $10,000 now is preferable. On the financial calculator, with $1,000 as the end-of-period PMT, 13 as n, and 4 as i, PVA = $9,985.65.

    (b) $10,000 in a lump sum now is even more preferable at the 6 percent discount rate. On the financial calculator, replace 4 with 6 as the i. PVA = $8,852.68.

12.   (a)   On the financial calculator, with $15,000 as the PV, 5 as the n, and 10 as the i, the end-of-year PMT = $3,956.96.

    (b) and (c) It is possible, though cumbersome, to create an amortization schedule such as the following, without using a financial calculator.

Year	(1) Unpaid Balance, Beg. of Year	(2) Payment, End of Year	(3) Interest Payment 10% x (1)	(4) Principal Payment (2)-(3)	(5) Unpaid Balance End of Year (1)-(4)
1	$15,000.00	$3,956.95	$1,500.00	$2,456.95	$12,543.05
2	$12,543.05	$3,956.95	$1,254.31	$2,702.64	$ 9,840.41
3	$ 9,840.41	$3,956.95	$ 984.04	$2,972.91	$ 6,867.50
4	$ 6,867.50	$3,956.95	$ 686.75	$3,270.20	$ 3,597.30
5	$ 3,597.30	$3,956.95	$ 359.73	$3,597.22	$ .08

Thus, the interest portion of the second payment will be $1,254.31, and the principal portion of the final payment will be $3,597.22. If you use the much faster financial calculator technique as described in the chapter, with $3,956.96 as the end-of-year PMT, the second interest payment is $1,254.30, and the final principal payment is $3,597.23.

13. On a financial calculator with $7,500 as the end-of-year PMT, $48,000 as the PV, and 13 as the i, you can find the precise n = 14.5952 (15 on the HP-12C).

14. Enter $10,000 as the PV, 3 as the n, and $4,199.31 as the end-of-year PMT in a financial calculator to find that i = 12.50000 percent.

15. On a financial calculator, enter $1,100 as the PV, $600 as the end-of-period PMT, 9 as the n, and 6 as the i to find the FV, $8,753.22.

Chapter Two

Time Value of Money: Advanced Concept and Applications

1.   The preceding chapter included explanations of how to compute the future value and present value of an annuity (or an annuity due). By definition of the term "annuity," the discussion dealt only with cases in which each of the payments or deposits in the series was of the same amount. The present chapter begins with an explanation of how to compute the present value and future value of a stream of *uneven* payments or deposits. The ability to do so will be useful in and of itself to solve several types of problems. It also is essential in order to evaluate various types of investments through discounted cash flow analysis, as will be explained later in this chapter.

PRESENT VALUE OF UNEVEN CASH FLOWS

2.   Assume that a young man will be entering college in one year. The estimated tuition is $6,000, to be paid at the start of the freshman year, $6,600 at the start of the sophomore year, $7,250 at the start of the junior year, and $8,100 at the start of the senior year. How much should be on hand today in an account earning 8.5 percent interest in order to just meet these four tuition payments as they come due? What is the present value of this series of uneven cash flows, discounted at 8.5 percent?

3.   The solution of a simple problem of this sort actually involves no techniques that have not already been covered earlier. All that is needed is to compute the present value of each of the four tuition payments and add them together. In other words, the present value of this stream of uneven payments is simply the sum of the present values of the four single sums.

4.   Since this sequence of cash flows is fairly brief, a simple tool such as a time value formula can be used to compute the present value fairly quickly.

End of Year	Tuition Amount	$\frac{1}{1.085^n}$	PVSS
1	$6,000	0.9217	$ 5,530.20
2	6,600	0.8495	5,606.70
3	7,250	0.7829	5,676.03
4	8,100	0.7216	5,844.96
	Total		$22,657.89

5.   If $22,657.89 is placed on deposit today, and if 8.5 percent compound interest is earned on the account balance over the next four years, there will be just enough to meet each of the estimated tuition payments as they fall due.   After the final payment is made, the account balance will be essentially zero. Table 2.1 shows the pattern of the account balance over the four years.

TABLE 2.1
Liquidation of a Capital Sum Compounding at 8.5% Interest Through Uneven Cash Withdrawals

Year	Beginning Balance	Interest Earnings	Cash With-drawal	Ending Balance
1	$22,657.89	$1,925.92	$6,000	$18,583.81
2	18,583.81	1,579.62	6,600	13,563.43
3	13,563.43	1,152.89	7,250	7,466.32
4	7,466.32	634.64	8,100	0.96

6.   This case is an illustration of so-called *ungrouped* cash flows, which means that the cash flow sequence includes no consecutive payments of the same amount and arithmetic sign, positive or negative. Each payment, therefore, has to be discounted separately. In some situations, however, there will also be some *grouped* cash flows, that is, some of the consecutive payments will be of the same amount and flow in

the same direction, either in or out. In this case, a shortcut is possible in finding the present value of the cash flows.

7.   A common example of an uneven cash flow where some of the payments can be grouped is a corporate bond. For example, assume that you are considering purchasing a bond that will pay you interest of $90 per year at the end of each of the next six years, as well as the $1,000 face amount at the end of the sixth year.[1] If you wish to earn a rate of return of 13 percent on your money, how much would you pay for the bond? That is, what is the present value, discounted at a 13 percent annual interest rate, of this income stream, which is depicted in figure 2.1?

Figure 2.1
Time Line Depiction of a Bond Value

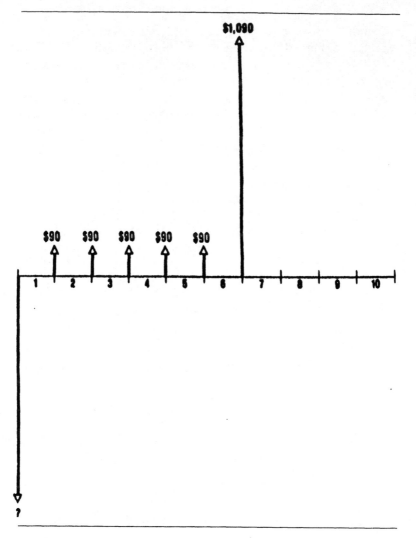

The time line depicts five annual payments of $90 each and a sixth of $1,090. The problem is to compute the present value of the stream of cash flows.

8.   This series of cash flows actually consists of two components: an annuity of $90 per year for five years and a single sum of $1,090 at the end of the sixth year (or an annuity of $90 per year for six years and a single sum of $1,000 at the end of the sixth year). Hence, to compute the present value of the entire sequence, it is necessary to: (a) compute the present value of the annuity, (b) compute the present value of the single sum, and (c) add the results together.

9.   Again, the sequence of cash flows is rather short and simple in the present illustration, so the solution can be calculated fairly quickly using time-value formulas. The PVA formula described in the previous chapter is:

$$PVA = \text{Annual payment} \times \left[\frac{1 - \frac{1}{(1+i)^n}}{i} \right]$$

In the present case, the PVA is:

$$PVA = \$90 \times \left[\frac{1 - \frac{1}{1.13^5}}{.13} \right]$$

$$= \$90 \times \left[\frac{1 - \frac{1}{1.18424}}{.13} \right]$$

$$= \$90 \times \left[\frac{1 - .5428}{.13} \right]$$

$$= \$90 \times \frac{.4572}{.13}$$

$$= \$90 \times 3.5169 = \$316.52$$

The PVSS is $\$1,090 \div 1.13^6 = \$1,090 \div 2.0820 = \$523.54$. Thus, the present value of the total sequence of cash flows, the price you would be willing to pay for the bond, is $840.06 ($316.52 + $523.54).

10.   To take a different situation involving some grouped cash flows, assume that you loan a sum of money to a borrower today. The repayment schedule calls for the borrower to make payments to you as follows:

End of Year	Payment Amount
1	$ 0
2	2,000
3-9	3,000
10	5,000

What is the present value of this sequence of payments, which is depicted in figure 2.2, if an 11 percent interest rate is assumed? In other words, how much would you be willing to lend?

FIGURE 2.2
Time Line Depiction of the Present Value of Uneven Cash Flows

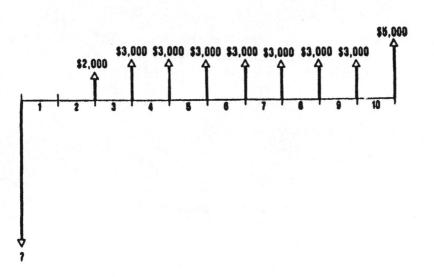

This time line shows a problem in which the task is to compute the present value of a stream of cash flows consisting of zero at the end of year one, $2,000 at the end of year two, $3,000 at the end of each of years three through nine, and $5,000 at the end of year ten.

11.   The solution to this problem involves several steps. First, the $2,000 payment at the end of year two must be discounted. Second, the present value of a seven-year $3,000 annuity must be computed. Third, the present value of that annuity must be further discounted as a single sum to compute its present value *today*, rather than its present value two years from now when the annuity begins. (Note that this annuity begins at the *start* of the third year, even though the first payment under it is not made until the *end* of the third year.) Fourth, the $5,000 payment at the end of year 10 must be

discounted. Finally, the PVSS of the first payment, the twice-discounted value of the PVA of the next seven payments, and the PVSS of the ninth payment must be added together to obtain the present value of the entire series of cash flows.

12.   Again, you can use the PVSS and PVA formulas to calculate all the values and total the results. The ambitious person who does so will find that the present value of this set of uneven cash flows is $14,858.98, as shown below.

(a)   PVSS of payment at end of year 2:

$$\frac{\$2,000}{1.11^2} \quad = \quad \frac{\$2,000}{1.2321} \quad = \quad \$1,623.24$$

(b)   PVA of payments at end of years 3-9:

$$\$3,000 \ \times \ \left[\frac{1 - \dfrac{1}{1.11^7}}{.11} \right]$$

$$\$3,000 \ \times \ \left[\frac{1 - \dfrac{1}{2.0762}}{.11} \right]$$

$$\$3,000 \ \times \ \frac{.5184}{.11}$$

$$\$3,000 \times 4.7127 = \$14,138.10$$

(c)   PVSS of PVA of payments at end of years 3-9:

$$\frac{\$14,138.10}{1.11^2} \quad = \quad \frac{\$14,138.10}{1.2321} \quad = \quad \$11,474.80$$

(d)   PVSS of payment at end of year 10:

$$\frac{\$5,000}{1.11^{10}} \quad = \quad \frac{\$5,000}{2.8394} \quad = \quad \$\,1,760.94$$

(e)   Total present value of the cash flows = $14,858.98

13.   One last point should be made before some slightly more complex cash flow patterns are taken up. In some problems, one or more of the cash flow amounts will be negative. For example, assume that you own rental property that is expected to generate net income for you of $15,000 per year at the end of each of the next 15 years, except for year 10. In that year, you estimate that replacement of the heating and air conditioning units will be necessary, causing a *net cash outflow* for the year of $6,000. What is the present value of this stream of cash flows, discounted at 9 percent?

14.   In this case, the only difference in procedure for finding the solution is that the present value of the net cash outflow must be *subtracted* from the aggregate present value of the net cash inflows. Specifically, in this illustration, the PVA and PVSS formulas could be used to produce the following approximate values:

(a)   PVA of inflows at end of years 1-9 $ 89,928
(b)   PVA of inflows at end of years 11-15   58,346
(c)   PVSS of PVA of inflows at end of years   24,645
(d)   Present value of cash inflows $114,573
(e)   PVSS of outflow at end of year 10   – 2,534
(f)   Present value of the net cash flows $112,039

15.   As you can see, the illustrations are becoming a bit complex, and the use of formulas to solve them is starting to be a little unwieldy. To reduce the difficulty, you may be able to express the cash flows of a problem in slightly different terms that are easier to deal with. For example, the preceding pattern of cash flows could have been expressed as:

(a)   An annuity of $15,000 for 15 years

(b)   An outflow of $21,000 at the end of year 10 (that is, $15,000 that needs to be subtracted out of the annuity and $6,000 that was the actual net outflow)

Calculation of the present value of this pattern of cash flows could have been completed in fewer steps than were presented above.

Using a Financial Calculator

16.   In all the illustrative problems up to this point, the solution could be found fairly easily because the pattern of payments was short and simple. Tools such as the time value formulas and a simple calculator suffice in such situations for computing and totalling the present value of the individual cash flows or, in the case of groups of level cash flows, the annuities.

17.   Often, however, a lengthy series of cash flows is involved in a problem. Also, frequently the series will involve many different payment amounts, some years of zero flows, and perhaps even some changes of arithmetic signs from positive to negative net flows and back again. For most such cases, a financial calculator like the HP-12C, HP-10B II, HP-17B II, or BA-II Plus is very well suited. For problems that exceed the usually ample capacity of these calculators, a computer program may be needed.

18.   First to be explained will be the use of these calculators to solve problems in which there are no consecutive cash flows that are of the same amount. In this case, the HP-12C has the capacity to solve problems involving up to 20 cash flows that occur at the end of each year (or 21 that occur at the beginning of each year). The HP-10B II has sufficient capacity to handle an initial cash flow and up to 14 cash flow groups, with up to 99 cash flows in each group. The HP-17B II has the capacity to solve problems with up to 700 separate uneven cash flows. The BA-II Plus has the capacity to handle up to 24 cash flows that occur at the end of each year (or 25 that occur at the beginning of each year).

19.   To illustrate, assume that an investment will produce the following pattern of net cash inflows during the next 20 years.

End of Year	Cash Flow	End of Year	Cash Flow
1	$ 500	11	$ 0
2	1,100	12	2,150
3	1,150	13	2,250
4	1,175	14	2,350
5	1,000	15	2,450
6	2,600	16	2,600
7	2,700	17	650
8	2,800	18	2,700
9	2,900	19	2,800
10	1,000	20	2,900

This set of data, together with the discount rate to be used, represents the maximum capacity that the HP-12C can handle, and almost all that the BA-II Plus can handle. It exceeds the capacity of the HP-10B II, whereas it barely scratches the surface of the HP-17B II's capacity. As will be explained below, a calculator's capacity can be expanded if some of the data consists of *grouped* data, that is, consecutive equal amounts with the same arithmetic sign, either plus or minus (for example, if each of the last three cash flows shown above were $2,800). Note in this problem, by the way, that some of the cash flows are of equal amounts (years six and 16, years seven and 18, years eight and 19, and years nine and 20). Nevertheless, these are not grouped data because the equal amounts do not occur in consecutive years.

Using the HP-12C

20. We will first take up problems entailing end-of-period cash flows. To solve a present value problem on the HP-12C, where the cash flows are ungrouped and begin one or more periods in the future, first look at the PMT key in the top row of the keyboard. Note that it also contains a blue CFj function. (The CFj symbol stands for juxtaposed, or side-by-side, cash flows.) This function will be used to enter the amount of each cash flow, including zero amounts. After all the payments in the series are entered, the discount rate will be entered with the i key as usual. Finally, note that the PV key in the top row of the keyboard also contains a yellow function, NPV, net present value. The yellow f key and NPV will be used to produce the solution.

21.   To illustrate the process, assume that you have a deferred compensation agreement with your employer. Under the agreement, the employer is obligated to pay you the following amounts:

End of year 1	$ 0
End of year 2	$75,000
End of year 3	$80,000
End of year 4	$85,000
End of year 5	$90,000

22.   If you use a discount rate of 12.5 percent, what is the present value of this future income stream? Press 0, blue g, and CFj. The initial year's zero value has now been entered. Press 75000, blue g, and CFj to reflect the amount to be received at the end of year two. Press 80000, blue g, and CFj to enter the cash inflow at the end of year three. Enter the remaining two payments by pressing 85000, blue g, CFj, 90000, blue g, and CFj. Now enter the discount rate by pressing 12.5 and the i key. Finally, compute the present value of the income stream by pressing the yellow f key and NPV. The answer, $218,454.50, appears on the display.

23.   Sometimes, you may want to view or revise the list of cash flows after they have been entered. To review the full list, press the RCL (for recall) key in the bottom row of the keyboard, blue g, and CFj. Do this repeatedly to show the cash flow amounts in reverse order, from last to first. To change a number in the list, key the new number into the display. Then press STO (in the bottom row of the keyboard) and the number of the cash flow to be replaced (beginning of year one is 0, end of year one is 1, end of year two is 2, and so on). Then recalculate the present value by pressing yellow f and NPV.

Using the HP-10B II

24.   To solve a present value problem on the HP-10B II where the cash flows are uneven and occur at the end of each period, we will use the calculator's cash flow application, which is triggered by the CFj key in the third row from the top of the keyboard, as well as the shift key and the NPV function on the PRC key.

25.   To illustrate, look at the brief series of cash flows in the deferred compensation agreement described in para. 21 above. If you use a 12.5 percent discount rate, what is the present value of this future income stream?   After clearing the calculator's memory, press the following keys: 0, CF$_j$ (to reflect the fact that there is no cash flow at the *start* of year one of the problem), 0, CF$_j$ (to reflect the fact that there is no cash flow at the *end* of year one of the problem), 75000, CF$_j$ (to enter the cash flow at the end of year two), 80000, CF$_j$ (to enter the cash flow at the end of year three), 85000, CF$_j$ (to enter the cash flow at the end of year four), 90000, CF$_j$ (to enter the cash flow at the end of year five), 12.5, I/YR (to enter the discount rate), shift, and NPV. The answer is $218,454.50.

26.   By the way, the $_j$ in CF$_j$ stands for the number of the cash flow. That, at the start of year one, is zero, and the subsequent cash flows (or groups of cash flows) are numbered consecutively, from one through as many as fourteen.

27.   A sometimes useful feature of the HP-10B II is that you can check or even alter the list of cash flows that have been entered. To view the list, press RCL (in the fourth row from the top of the keyboard), CF$_j$ 0 (to recall the initial cash flow), RCL, CF$_j$, + (to recall the next cash flow), RCL, CF$_j$, + (to recall the next cash flow), and so on through the list. To replace a number in the list, recall that cash flow, enter the new cash flow, and press shift, STO (on the RCL key), CF$_j$, and the number of the cash flow being replaced. Then press shift, NPV to find the present value of the revised set of cash flows. It isn't possible to add or eliminate cash flows on this calculator, so if this is the objective, it will be necessary to clear the machine and start over.

Using the HP-17B II

28.   To solve a present value problem on the HP-17B II, where the cash flows are uneven and occur at the end of each period, we will use the calculator's CFLO (cash flow) menu, which you will find at the same level in the menu system as the TVM menu. Press the CFLO menu key, shift, CLEAR DATA, and the YES menu key. Then press the #T? menu key. If the Time Prompting function is shown to be OFF, release the key. If not, press the #T? menu again to shut it off. Now you are ready to enter a series of ungrouped cash flows and compute their present value.

29.   To illustrate the process, look at the brief series of cash flows in the deferred compensation agreement described in para. 21 above. The HP-17B II is asking you for FLOW(0), which is the cash flow at the *start* of year one of the problem. Since there is nothing at that time in the problem you are considering, press 0 and INPUT. The calculator now is asking you for FLOW(1), which is the cash flow at the *end* of year one. Since this too is zero, press 0 and INPUT. The calculator then asks for the next cash flow, so press 75000 and INPUT. For the remaining cash flows press 80000, INPUT, 85000, INPUT, 90000, and INPUT. Now that the full series of cash flows is in the machine, press EXIT and the CALC menu key. Before you can compute the (net) present value of the series, you must tell the machine what discount rate to use. Press 12.5 and the I% menu key. Then press the NPV menu key to find the answer, $218,454.50[2].

30.   A sometimes useful feature of the HP-17B II is that is enables the user to check or even to alter the list of cash flows that have been entered. To review the amount of each of the flows, starting at the end of the series and proceeding back to the beginning, press the EXIT key and then press the up arrow key in the left-hand column of the keyboard several times. To change the amount of one of the cash flows, use the down or up arrow keys to display the item to be changed. Then key in the new value, press INPUT, and recompute the NPV. To delete a cash flow from the list, display the item to be eliminated and press the DELET menu key and recompute the NPV. To insert an additional cash flow, display the cash flow that follows the new one. Press the INSR menu key; then key in the new value, press INPUT, and recompute the NPV.

Using the BA-II Plus

31.   If you wish to solve a present value problem on the BA-II Plus, where the cash flows are uneven and occur at the end of each period, you will need to again use the prompted-worksheet mode. This time, however, you will not be using the amortization worksheet explained in Chapter One. Instead, you will use the cash flows worksheet, which can be accessed through the CF key in the second row of the keyboard. You will also use the NPV key in the same row of the keyboard to calculate the net present value of the cash flow.

32.   To illustrate, look at the brief series of cash flows in the deferred compensation agreement described in para. 21 above. If you use a 12.5 percent discount rate, what is the present value of this future income stream? Press the following keys:

CF, 2nd, CLR Work	(to enter the cash flows prompted worksheet and clear it of extraneous data)
ENTER, ↓	(because there is no cash flow at the start of year 1)
0, ENTER, ↓, ↓	(because there is no cash flow at the end of year 1 and to prepare to enter the next cash flow)
75000, ENTER, ↓, ↓	(to enter the first cash flow, to show that it occurred only once, and to prepare to enter the next cash flow)
80000, ENTER, ↓, ↓	(to enter the second cash flow, to show that it occurred only once, and to prepare to enter the next cash flow)
85000, ENTER, ↓, ↓	(to enter the third cash flow, to show that it occurred only once, and to prepare to enter the next cash flow)
90000, ENTER, ↓, ↓	(to enter the final cash flow, to show that it occurred only once, and to prepare to solve the problem)
NPV, 12.5, ENTER, ↓	(to tell the machine that you want to find the net present value of these cash flows discounted at 12.5 percent)
CPT	(to produce the answer)

The answer, $218,454.50, will appear on the display.

33.   Sometimes, it is useful to be able to review the cash flows that have been entered or even to revise one or more of them. To see the list again, press the CF key and move through the list by pressing the down arrow key several times. To remove a number from the list, display that number and press 2nd, DEL. Then recompute the NPV. To insert a number into the list,

display the space where it is to be inserted. Press 2nd, INS, the number to be inserted, and ENTER. Then recompute the NPV.

34.   These four calculators can solve present value problems involving a great many cash flows if the series includes some grouped data because grouped data count as only one cash flow *amount*. For example, a cash flow of $50,000, followed by 40 annual cash flows of $2,000, involves 41 cash flows but only two cash flow amounts. For problems that include grouped data, you should enter, along with the amount of each such cash flow, the total number of times it occurs in succession, including the first time. On the HP-12C, this number is entered by means of the blue Nj function on the FV key in the center of the top row of the keyboard. On the HP-10B II, this number is entered by means of the shift key and the N_j function on the CF$_j$ key. On the HP-17B II, this number is entered after you have turned the #T? function to ON. On the BA-II Plus, this number is entered when you respond to the FO= prompt that appears on the display after each cash flow (other than the first one) is entered.

35.   To illustrate the process, assume that you are considering investing in a "great opportunity" that will yield a cash inflow to you, starting next year, of $6,000 per year for five years, followed by $4,000 per year for ten years, followed by $2,000 per year for 15 years, followed by a lump-sum payment one year later of $25,000. Compute the present value of this income stream, utilizing an 8 percent discount rate.

36.   On the HP-12C, begin by entering the amount of the initial inflow: 6000, blue g, and CFj. Since it will occur a total of five times (including the first), press 5, blue g, and Nj. Now enter the next group of inflows: 4000, blue g, CFj, and the number of times this amount will occur: 10, blue g, Nj. Enter the third group of inflows by pressing 2000, blue g, CFj, 15, blue g, and Nj. Then enter the final inflow, 25000, blue g, CFj. Finally, enter the interest rate by pressing 8 and i. Compute the answer by pressing yellow f and NPV, and the answer, $49,920.35, appears on the screen. You can revise the interest rate if you wish simply by entering the new rate and pressing i, yellow f, and NPV.

37.   On the HP-10B II, press 0, CF$_j$ (since there is no cash flow at the *start* of year one). Then press 6000 and CF$_j$. Since it will occur a total of five times (including the first), press 5, shift,

and N_j. Now enter the next group of cash flows: 4000, CF_j, and the number of times this amount will occur: 10, shift, and N_j. Enter the third group of cash flows: 2000, CF_j, 15, shift, and N_j. Then enter the final cash flow: 25000 and CF_j. Finally, enter the interest rate: 8 and I/YR. Compute the answer, $49,920.35, by pressing shift and NPV. You can revise the interest rate if you wish simply by entering the new rate, I/YR, and pressing shift and NPV.

38.   If you are using the HP-17B II, enter the cash flow mode by pressing the CFLO menu key and clear its memory. Press the #T? menu key once or twice to turn the function that prompts you to tell how many times a particular cash flow occurs to ON. Next, press 0 and INPUT to tell the machine that there is no cash flow at the start of the first year. Now press 6000, INPUT, 5, and INPUT to tell the machine that the first cash flow is $6,000 and that it occurs for five consecutive periods. Then press 4000, INPUT, 10, and INPUT to enter the next set of cash flows. Complete the series by pressing 2000, INPUT, 15, INPUT, 25000, INPUT, 1, and INPUT. Now press EXIT, the CALC menu key, 8, the I% menu key, and the NPV menu key to produce the answer, $49,920.35. You can revise the interest rate if you wish by simply entering the new rate and pressing the I% and the NPV menu keys.

39.   The present value of this same "great opportunity" can be solved with the BA-II Plus by pressing the following keys:

CF, 2nd, CLR Work, ENTER, ↓	(to clear the worksheet, to show that there is no cash flow at the start of the first year, and to prepare to enter the first set of cash flows)
6000, ENTER, ↓, 5, ENTER, ↓	(to enter the first set of 5 cash flows)
4000, ENTER, ↓, 10, ENTER, ↓	(to enter this set of 10 cash flows)
2000, ENTER, ↓, 15, ENTER, ↓	(to enter this set of 15 cash flows)
25000, ENTER, ↓, ↓	(to enter the final lump-sum payment and to prepare to solve the problem)
NPV, 8, ENTER, ↓, CPT	(to calculate the answer at the specified discount rate)

The answer is shown as $49,920.35. You can revise the interest rate if you wish by pressing NPV, the new interest rate, ENTER, ↓, and CPT.

40.   Each of the preceding illustrations of how to use the HP-12C, HP-10B II HP-17B II, and BA-II Plus involved cash flows that occurred at the end of the year. If the cash flows occur at the beginning of the year, only a slight change in procedure is needed to find the present value of the payment stream.[3]

41.   If you are using the HP-12C, take another look at the PV key, and note that it has a blue CFo function. If the problem to be solved entails cash flows at the beginning of each year, the first such flow (or group of consecutive cash inflows or outflows of equal amount) is entered by means of this blue CFo function. (The symbol CFo stands for original cash flow.) Subsequent cash flows are then entered via the CFj function in the manner described above.

42.   If your calculator is the HP-10B II, simply press the amount of the initial cash flow (if it occurs only once, that is, if it is ungrouped data), CF$_j$, and then proceed in the manner described above to enter the size and number of each of the remaining cash flows. However, if the first cash flow consists of grouped data, for example, $1,000 at the beginning of years one,

two, three, and four, the data must be treated as two separate cash flows, $1,000 occurring at the start of the first year followed by a group of three additional cash flows of $1,000 each.

43.   If you are using the HP-17B II, notice that when you enter the cash flow made by pressing the CFLO menu key, the calculator asks for the FLOW(0), the original cash flow, the cash flow at the start of the first year. If this cash flow is ungrouped data, enter the first cash flow here and proceed in the manner described above to enter the size and number of each of the subsequent cash flows. However, if the first cash flow constitutes grouped data, for example, $1,000 at the beginning of years one, two, three, and four, this data must be treated as two separate cash flows, $1,000 occurring at the start of the first year followed by a group of three additional cash flows of $1,000 each.

44.   If you are using the BA-II Plus, notice that when you enter the cash flow prompted worksheet, the calculator asks for the CFo, the original cash flow. If this cash flow is ungrouped data, insert the first cash flow here and proceed in the manner described above to enter the size and number of each of the subsequent cash flows. However, if the first cash flow constitutes grouped data, for example, $1,000 at the beginning of years one, two, three, and four, this data must be treated as two separate cash flows, $1,000 occurring at the start of year one followed by a group of three additional cash flows of $1,000 each.

45.   To illustrate, if a 12 percent discount rate is used, what is the present value of the following series of cash flows?

Beginning of Year	Amount
1-5	$3,500
6-10	2,500
11	1,500
12	500

46.   On the HP-12C, enter the first five cash flows by pressing 3500, blue g, CFo, 5, blue g, and Nj. The next five cash flows are entered by pressing 2500, blue g, CFj, 5, blue g, and

Nj. The last two cash flows are entered by pressing 1500, blue g, CFj, 500, blue g, and CFj. The solution is found by entering the discount rate (12 and i) and pressing yellow f and NPV. The answer, $20,484.67, appears on the display.

47.   On the HP-10B II, after clearing the machine's memory of any old data, enter the first five cash flows by pressing 3500, CF_j, 3500, CF_j, 4, shift, and N_j. The next five cash flows are entered by pressing 2500, CF_j, 5, shift, and N_j. The last two cash flows are entered by pressing 1500, CF_j, 500, and CF_j. The answer is then found by pressing 12, I/YR, shift, and NPV. The display screen shows $20,484.67.

48.   On the HP-17B II, after entering the cash flow menu system and clearing CFLO of any old data, turn on the #T? function. Enter the cash flows by pressing 3500, INPUT, 3500, INPUT, 4, INPUT, 2500, INPUT, 5, INPUT, 1500, INPUT 1, INPUT, 500, INPUT, 1, and INPUT. Next, press EXIT the CALC menu key, 12, the I% menu key, and NPV. The answer, $20,484.67, will be displayed.

49.   On the BA-II Plus, after entering the cash flow prompted worksheet and clearing it of any old data, enter the first five cash flows by pressing 3500, ENTER, ↓, 3500, ENTER, ↓, 4, ENTER, and ↓. The next five cash flows are then entered by pressing 2500, ENTER, ↓, 5, ENTER, and ↓. The last two cash flows are entered by pressing 1500, ENTER, ↓, ↓, 500, ENTER, ↓, and ↓. The solution is then found by pressing NPV, 12, ENTER, ↓, and CPT. The answer, $20,484.67, appears on the display.

Payments Growing by a Constant Percentage

50.   In many cases, time value of money problems involve the need to discount to their present value a stream of payments that grow by a constant annual percentage. Such payments are sometimes called *serial payments*. Adjusting for an assumed inflation rate is often the underlying motivation for using serial payments.

51.   For example, assume that you wish to have an income stream of $25,000 per year *in constant purchasing power* for each of the next ten years, starting immediately. How large a capital sum would you need to set aside today to meet this

objective if the annual inflation rate is assumed to be 5 percent and if the principal sum to be liquidated can be assumed to produce a rate of return of 8 percent per year? What is the present value, discounted at 8 percent, of this ten-year stream of payments that will rise by 5 percent per year?

52.   You could, of course, calculate the amount of each of the 10 payments, discount each of them for the appropriate number of years, and add up the results. There is, however, a better way to produce the answer to this problem. If done manually, it involves using the following formula:

$$PV = (1 + i) \left[\frac{1 - \left[\frac{(1 + \text{Growth rate})}{(1 + i)}\right]^n}{(i - \text{Growth rate})} \right] \text{Amount of 1st payment}$$

In the present illustration, the answer is:

$$= \quad 1.08 \times \left[\frac{1 - \left[\frac{1.05}{1.08}\right]^{10}}{(.08 - .05)} \right] \times \$25,000$$

$$= \quad 1.08 \times \left[\frac{1 - .7545}{.03} \right] \times \$25,000$$

$$= \quad 1.08 \times 8.1836 \times \$25,000$$

$$= \quad \$220,957.20$$

If the first $25,000 payment is to be made after one year, rather than immediately, the answer found through this formula should be divided by $(1 + i)$. In this case, the present value would be ($220,957.20 ÷ 1.08 =) $204,590.00.

53.   Rather than laboring through the formula, you may prefer to use a financial calculator to solve this type of problem. On the HP-12C, the keystrokes would be as follows for the beginning-of-year approach:

blue g, BEG, 25000, PMT   (to enter the first payment,
                                 which is to occur
                                 immediately)
1.08, ENTER, 1.05, ÷, 1,   (to enter the inflation-
–, 100, x, i   adjusted discount rate)
10, n, PV   (to enter the n and produce the
                                 solution)

The answer, $220,955.95, will appear on the display. Dividing this result by 1.08 will produce the end-of-year solution, $204,588.85.

54.   Or, on the HP-10B II, set the calculator for beginning-of-period payments. Then press 25000, PMT (to enter the first payment). Next, press 1.08, ÷, 1.05, –, 1, x, 100, =, I/YR (to enter the inflation-adjusted interest rate). Then press 10, N, and PV (to enter the number of periods and produce the solution). The answer is $220,955.95. If you want to see the answer under an end-of-period assumption, divide this answer by 1.08. Press ÷, 1.08, =. The revised answer is $204,588.85.

55.   If you are using the HP-17B II, return to the TVM menu system by pressing shift, MAIN, the FIN menu key, and the TVM menu key. Set the calculator for beginning-of-period payments. Then press the following keys: 25000, the PMT menu key, 1.08, ÷, 1.05, –, 1, x, 100, =, and the I%YR menu key. You have now entered the initial payment and the inflation-adjusted discount rate. Now press 10, the N menu key, and the PV menu key to produce the solution, $220,955.95. If you want to see the answer under the assumption of end-of-period payments, divide this answer by 1.08. Press ÷, 1.08, =, and the revised answer, $204,588.85, will appear on the display.

56.   On the BA-II Plus, return to the standard-calculator mode by pressing 2nd and QUIT. Set the calculator for beginning-of-period payments. Clear the calculator of extraneous data by pressing 2nd and CLR TVM. Then the keystrokes for the beginning-of-year solution would be as follows:

25000, PMT   (to enter the first payment)
1.08, ÷, 1.05, –, 1,   (to enter the inflation-
x, 100, =, I/Y   adjusted discount rate)
10, N, CPT, PV   (to enter the N and produce
                            the solution)

The answer, $220,955.95, will appear on the display. Dividing this result by 1.08 will produce the end-of-year solution, $204,588.85.

FUTURE VALUE OF UNEVEN CASH FLOWS

57.   The following pages deal with the reverse of the previous set of problems and explain how to calculate the future value of a series of uneven cash flows. The explanation can be brief because the approach to solving such problems parallels that for solving present value problems.

58.   Assume that a business plans to make the following series of contributions to fund certain obligations under its pension plan:

End of Year	Amount
1	$30,000
2	40,000
3-5	50,000
6-10	60,000

If these contributions are credited with 10 percent interest per year, how much will be in the fund at the end of the tenth year? What is the future value of this series of uneven cash flows? The solution of this type of problem entails compounding each payment from the time it is made until the end of the tenth year and totalling the results. Thus, the first $30,000 should be compounded for nine years at 10 percent to produce its FVSS. The second should be compounded for eight years, the third for seven years, etc. The final $60,000 payment, of course, earns no interest because it is made at the end of the tenth year.

Using Time-Value Formulas

59.   If, as in the present illustration, the sequence of cash flows is brief and straightforward, the basic future value formulas can be used to produce a solution. Specifically, the future value of this series of uneven cash flows at 10 percent can be found by the really ambitious TVM student as shown below.[4]

(a)   FVSS of payment at end of year 1

$$\$30,000 \times 1.10^9 = \qquad \$ 70,738.43$$

(b)   FVSS of payment at end of year 2

$$\$40,000 \times 1.10^8 = \qquad 85,743.55$$

(c)   FVA of payments at end of years 3-5

$$\$50,000 \times \left[\frac{1.10^3 - 1}{.10}\right]$$

$$= \$165,500$$

(d)   FVSS of FVA of payments at end of years 3-5

$$\$165,500 \times 1.10^5 = \qquad 266,539.41$$

(e)   FVA of payments at end of years 6-10

$$\$60,000 \times \left[\frac{1.10^5 - 1}{.10}\right] = \quad 366,306.00$$

(f)   Future value of the cash flows $789,327.39

Using a Financial Calculator

60.   The HP-12C, HP-10B II, and BA-II Plus calculators are not constructed to compute *directly* the future value of a series of uneven cash flows. However, since they do have the capability to compute the *present* value of a series of uneven cash flows, you can compute the single sum that is the present value of the cash flows and then compute the *future* value of that single sum. This provides the same result as if you calculated the future value of the cash flows directly. The HP-17B II, unlike the other machines, can produce the answer directly.

61.   For example, assume the following sequence of cash flows:

End of Year	Amount
1	$500
2-5	600
6-8	700

Calculate the future value as of the end of year eight using a 7 percent interest rate.

Using the HP-12C

62.   On the HP-12C, begin by computing the present value of these cash flows as explained earlier. Press the keys as shown below.

> 500, blue g, CFj
> 600, blue g, CFj, 4, blue g, Nj
> 700, blue g, CFj, 3, blue g, Nj
> 7, i, yellow f, NPV

The present value, $3,676.43, appears on the display. Now carry this present value forward as a single sum to the end of year eight, using the same 7 percent interest rate by pressing the following keys:

> CHS, PV, 8, n, FV

The future value of this series of uneven cash flows, $6,316.79, appears on the display. If the cash flows in this problem had occurred at the beginning of each year, rather than the end, you would use the same procedure, but multiply the answer by (1 plus the interest rate).

Using the HP-10B II

63.   If your calculator is the HP-10B II, begin by computing the present value of these cash flows as explained earlier. Press the following keys:

$$0, CF_j, 500, CF_j$$
$$600, CF_j, 4, shift, N_j$$
$$700, CF_j, 3, shift, N_j$$
$$7, I/YR, shift, NPV$$

The present value, \$3,676.43, appears on the display. Now carry this present value forward as a single sum to the end of year eight, using the same 7 percent interest rate by pressing the following keys:

+/-, PV, 8, N, FV

The future value of this set of uneven cash flows is \$6,316.79. If the cash flows in this problem had occurred at the beginning of each year, rather than at the end, you would use the same procedure, but multiply the answer by (1 plus the interest rate).

Using the BA-II Plus

64.   Or, if you are using the BA-II Plus, compute the present value of the cash flows by pressing the following keys:

CF, 2nd, CLR Work, ENTER, ↓,
500, ENTER, ↓, ↓,
600, ENTER, ↓, 4, ENTER, ↓,
700, ENTER, ↓, 3, ENTER, ↓,
NPV, 7, ENTER, ↓, CPT

The present value, \$3,676.43, will appear on the display. Now carry this present value forward as a single sum to the end of year eight using the same 7 percent interest rate by pressing the following keys:

STO, 1	(to store this present value in a memory register)
2nd, QUIT, 2nd, CLR TVM	(to leave the prompted-worksheet mode, return to the standard-calculator mode, and clear the calculator of extraneous data)
RCL, 1, +/-, PV	(to recall the stored value and enter it as a negative present value)
8, N, 7, I/Y	(to insert the rest of the information needed to find the future value)

CPT, FV   (to produce the answer)

The future value, $6,316.79, will appear on the display. If the cash flows in this problem had occurred at the beginning of each year, rather than the end, you would use the same procedure, but multiply the answer by (1 plus the interest rate).

Using the HP-17B II

65.   On the HP-17B II, solving a future-value-of-uneven-cash-flows problem is less cumbersome. Enter the CFLO mode and clear the CFLO memory of any extraneous data. Turn the #T? function to ON. Then press the following keys:

0, INPUT,
500, INPUT, 1, INPUT,
600, INPUT, 4, INPUT,
700, INPUT, 3, INPUT,
EXIT, the CALC menu key,
7, the I% menu key, and the NFV menu key

The answer, $6,316.79, will appear on the display. If the cash flows in this problem had occurred at the beginning of each year, rather than the end, you could use the same procedure, but multiply the answer by (1 plus the interest rate).

Deposits Growing by a Constant Percentage

66.   Now, instead of dealing with the future value of cash flows that change in an irregular manner, we will take up the case of the future value of cash flows whose amounts increase each year by a constant percentage.   This type of problem frequently arises where someone sets up a savings plan for the attainment of a financial goal and where the amount to be saved each year rises at about the same constant rate as the person's income is expected to grow.

67.   For example, assume that you plan to begin a program of annual saving, beginning with a $500 deposit now. Assume also that you expect your income and, hence, the amount you can save to rise by about 10 percent per year. If your savings generate a 7 percent annual rate of return, how much will be in your account at the end of five years? What is the future value,

compounded at 7 percent interest, of this five-year stream of deposits that will rise by 10 percent per year?

68.   You could, of course, calculate the amount of each of the five deposits, compound each of them for the appropriate number of years, and add up the results. There is, however, a faster way. This type of problem can be solved through the use of the following formula where the first deposit is made immediately.

$$FV = (1 + i) \left[\frac{(1 + i)^n - (1 + \text{Growth rate})^n}{(i - \text{Growth rate})} \right] \text{Amount of 1st deposit}$$

In the present example, the answer is:

$$= \quad (1.07) \quad \times \quad \left[\frac{(1.07)^5 - (1.10)^5}{(.07 - .10)} \right] \times \$500$$

$$= \quad (1.07) \quad \times \quad \left[\frac{1.4026 - 1.6105}{-.03} \right] \times \$500$$

$$= \quad 1.07 \times 6.9319 \times \$500$$

$$= \quad \$3,708.57$$

If the first $500 deposit is to be made after one year, rather than immediately, the answer found through this formula should be divided by (1 + i). In this case, the future value would be ($3,708.59 ÷ 1.07 =) $3,465.00.

69.   If instead of using the formula, you prefer a financial calculator for solving this type of problem, the HP-12C, HP-10B II, HP-17B II, or BA-II Plus can be used. However, they can compute the solution only in an indirect manner. First, compute the present value and then carry this amount forward as a single sum to the end of the compounding period.

70.   The HP-12C keystrokes needed to solve the present problem, based on the beginning-of-period approach, are as follows:

blue g, BEG, 500, PMT	(to enter the first deposit)
1.07, ENTER, 1.10, ÷,	(to enter the inflation-
1, –, 100, x, i	adjusted discount rate)
5, n, PV	(to enter the number of payments and produce the present value)
7, i, 0, PMT	(to restore the original compounding rate and to clear the extraneous data)
FV	(to produce the solution)

The answer, $3,708.59, will appear on the display. Dividing the result by 1.07 will produce the end-of-year solution, $3,465.97.

71.   On the HP-10B II, clear the memory and set the machine for beginning-of-period payments or deposits. Then press the following keys:

500, PMT	(to enter the first deposit)
1.07, ÷, 1.10, –, 1	(to enter the inflation-
x, 100, =, I/YR	adjusted interest rate)
5, N, PV	(to enter the number of payments and produce the present value)
7, I/YR, 0, PMT	(to restore the original compounding rate and clear out the extraneous data)
FV	(to produce the solution)

The answer is $3,708.59. Dividing this result by 1.07 will produce the end-of-period solution, $3,465.97.

72.   On the HP-17B II, enter the TVM menu system, clear any extraneous data, and set the machine for the beginning-of-period mode. Then press the following keys:

500, the PMT menu key	(to enter the first deposit)
1.07, ÷, 1.10, –, 1, x,	(to enter the inflation-
100, =, the I%YR menu key	adjusted discount rate)
5, the N menu key, the PV menu key	(to enter the number of payments and produce the present value)
7, the I%YR menu key	(to restore the original compounding rate)

| 0, the PMT menu key | (to clear out the extraneous data) |
| the FV menu key | (to produce the solution) |

The answer, $3,708.59, will appear on the display. Dividing this result by 1.07 will produce the end-of-period solution, $3,465.97.

73.   On the BA-II Plus, begin by clearing the TVM registers and setting the calculator for beginning-of-period deposits or payments. Then press the following keys:

500, PMT	(to enter the first deposit)
1.07, ÷, 1.10, –, 1,	(to enter the inflation-
x, 100, =, I/Y	adjusted discount rate)
5, N, CPT, PV	(to enter the number of payments and produce the present value)
7, I/Y, 0, PMT	(to restore the original compounding rate and clear out the extraneous data)
CPT, FV	(to produce the solution)

The answer, $3,708.59, will appear on the display. Dividing this result by 1.07 will produce the end-of-period solution, $3,465.97.

EVALUATING AN INVESTMENT THROUGH DISCOUNTED CASH FLOW ANALYSIS

74.   One of the most common personal and business applications of time-value-of-money principles and techniques is the evaluation of a proposed investment. For example, assume that you are considering the purchase of a bond that will involve a cash outlay now (the purchase price) and a series of cash inflows over several time periods in the future (the interest payments and the face amount). Or, perhaps you are considering construction of an apartment building that will involve a cash outlay now and perhaps again next year (the construction costs), after which you anticipate a series of cash inflows for a period of years (the rental payments). Or, perhaps the investment under consideration is the purchase (cash outflow) of a piece of equipment that will reduce expenses (cash "inflow") over some future time period.

75.   In all of these types of situations there is a trade-off: one or more cash outflows in return for one or more cash inflows. The question: are the inflows to be received worth the outflows that will be expended? Is it a good investment? By this point, you surely understand that the question cannot be adequately answered without taking into account the time value of money. Discounted cash flow analysis assists you to evaluate an investment by making comparable the time value of the cash outflows and the time value of the cash inflows. It thus can be used to assist in deciding: (a) whether or not a proposed investment project is an acceptable one, and (b) how to rank several competing investment opportunities in terms of their relative acceptability.

76.   Of course, there is more to evaluating an investment than simply crunching some numbers through various time-value-of-money formulas, tables, or calculator functions. The degree of certainty or uncertainty associated with the various cash outflows and inflows, both in amount, timing, and duration, as well as the tax aspects, also must be considered. Evaluation of the tax elements is beyond the scope of this book. Risk considerations, however, are incorporated in the interest rate that is used in discounted cash flow analysis.

77.   As you will see, the mechanics of discounted cash flow analysis are quite straightforward when the pattern of the cash outflows and inflows is simple. Life becomes a bit more complex when the amounts of each vary from year to year, and still more complex when the combined effect of the outflows and inflows begins switching from negative to positive to negative to positive, back and forth, from year to year. Some simple situations will be dealt with first, followed by gradually more complicated cases.

Discounted Cash Flow Techniques Defined

78.   There are two commonly used techniques for discounted cash flow analysis: calculation of an investment's net present value (NPV) and its internal rate of return (IRR).

Net Present Value

79.   The net present value of an investment is defined as the present value of the stream of cash inflows, minus the present

value of the stream of cash outflows, with both present values calculated on the basis of an appropriate rate of interest. The discount rate used might be the minimum rate of return that is acceptable to the investor in light of his or her assessment of the riskiness of the investment, the cost of the capital the investor would have to raise in order to make the investment, or the rate available on another acceptable investment being considered that involves a similar degree of riskiness.

80.   If the result of the NPV calculation is positive, that is, if the present value of the inflow stream exceeds the present value of the outflow stream, the investment is a good one. The investment provides a net addition to the wealth (in a time-value sense) of the investor in the amount of the positive remainder. A positive NPV means that the rate of return provided by the investment (whatever that rate is) exceeds the discount rate being used as the benchmark. If the NPV is negative, the reverse is true, and the investment will result in a net reduction in the wealth (in a time-value sense) of the investor. And if the NPV is zero, the investment will neither add to nor subtract from the investor's wealth (in a time-value sense), so that it is a matter of indifference as to whether the investment should be made.

Internal Rate of Return

81.   The internal rate of return on an investment is the interest rate that equates the present value of the stream of cash inflows to the present value of the stream of cash outflows. If that rate is larger than the minimum rate deemed acceptable by the investor, the investment is a good one and should be pursued. If not, it should be rejected. The criteria for determining the acceptable minimum rate of return are the same as those described in connection with the net present value technique.

Similarity of the NPV and IRR Techniques

82.   Note that these two methods of evaluating an investment are very similar. In computing NPV, the investor specifies the minimum acceptable interest rate and determines whether, at that rate, the present value of the inflows exceeds the present value of the outflows. In computing IRR, the investor computes the interest rate that will make the present value of the inflows equal

to the present value of the outflows; that is, the investor computes the interest rate that will produce an NPV of zero.

83.   As a general rule, when used to evaluate a particular investment, the two techniques will lead the investor to the same conclusion if the same data are used. If the NPV is positive, the IRR normally will be acceptable, and the investment will be an attractive one. Conversely, if the NPV is negative, the IRR normally will be unacceptable, and the investment should be rejected. When used to *rank* several investments as to their *relative* acceptability, however, there are situations in which the NPV and IRR techniques can produce different results using the same data, as will be explained later in this chapter. In most cases, the NPV method is more reliable for purposes of ranking several competing investment possibilities. The project with the largest NPV should be ranked first, the one with the next largest NPV should be ranked second, and so on.

Computing Net Present Value: Simple Problems

84.   Consider the following, very simple investment. You are evaluating the purchase of a piece of equipment that will cost $10,000. It will provide a net cash flow of $4,000 per year at the end of each of the next four years, after which it will have no value. If your cost of capital is 10 percent per year, is this a worthwhile investment?[5]

85.   Depicted on a time line, the cash flows associated with this project appear as shown in the upper half of figure 2.3. The single component of cash outflow, $10,000, occurs immediately, so its present value is a negative $10,000. The four inflows of $4,000 each, totalling $16,000, constitute a four-year annuity, to be discounted at 10 percent. You have already learned how to calculate a PVA by means of a formula, as follows:

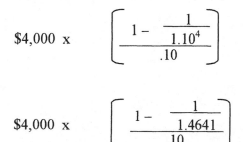

$$\$4,000 \times \left[\frac{1 - \dfrac{1}{1.10^4}}{.10} \right]$$

$$\$4,000 \times \left[\frac{1 - \dfrac{1}{1.4641}}{.10} \right]$$

$$\$4,000 \times \frac{.3170}{.10}$$

$$\$4,000 \times 3.1700 = \$12,680.00$$

Subtracting the present value of the outflow, $10,000, you find that the project has a positive NPV of $2,679.60. Your wealth will be increased (in a time-value sense) by this amount if you invest in the project. So far, then, the calculation of NPV involves nothing that you have not already learned to do.

86.   And, if the problem is made a bit more complex by changing it to one involving uneven cash flows, the calculation still is similar to those explained earlier. The lower half of figure 2.3 shows a modification to the preceding case by including a pattern of increasing cash inflows totalling the same $16,000. The present value of the income stream depicted there, discounted at 10 percent, can be found by the method described earlier. For example, using the basic formula to compute a PVSS, you can find the present value of each inflow and total them to produce the solution.

FIGURE 2.3
Time Line Representation of NPV Problem: Level and Uneven
Inflows

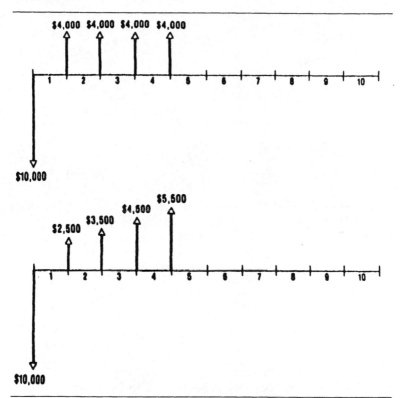

The upper time line depicts an investment that entails an initial
cash outflow of $10,000 and a level stream of four $4,000 cash
inflows. In the lower time line, the initial cash outflow is the
same, but the four cash inflows follow an increasing pattern over
time.

Amount	x	$\frac{1}{(1+i)^n} =$	PVSS
$2,500		$\frac{1}{(1.10)}$	$2,272.73
$3,500		$\frac{1}{(1.10)^2}$	2,892.56
$4,500		$\frac{1}{(1.10)^3}$	3,380.92
$5,500 Total		$\frac{1}{(1.10)^4}$	3,756.57 $12,302.78

87.   Subtracting the present value of the outflow stream, $10,000, you find that this investment has a positive net present value of $2,302.78. (It should not be surprising that the NPV with the increasing pattern of cash inflows, $2,302.78, is less than the NPV for the previous case of level cash inflows, $2,679.60, that totalled the same amount, $16,000.)

88.   An additional level of complexity can be introduced into the problem if it is assumed that a *series* of cash outflows is required before the series of cash inflows begins. See, for example, figure 2.4, in which the top time line depicts a project calling for three years of uneven cash outflows ($2,000, $1,000, and $500), followed by five years of cash inflows ($500, $1,000, $2,000, $2,000, and $3,000). Here, the only new procedure is that you must subtract the present value of the *series* of outflows from the present value of the series of inflows. Note also from the time line when the outflows are assumed to occur (at the *beginning* of years one, two, and three) and when the inflows are assumed to occur (at the *end* of years three, four, five, six, and seven).

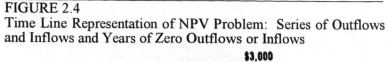

FIGURE 2.4
Time Line Representation of NPV Problem: Series of Outflows and Inflows and Years of Zero Outflows or Inflows

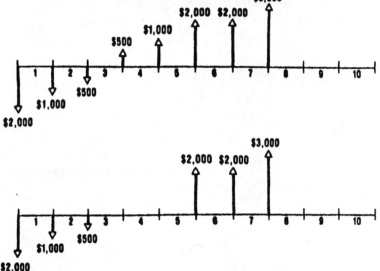

The top line depicts an investment that entails a decreasing series of cash outflows followed by an increasing series of cash inflows. The lower line depicts a similar situation, except that there is a gap of three years between the last outflow and the first inflow.

89.   Based on the use of the PVSS formula, the procedure for finding the solution to this problem, with a discount rate of, for example, 8 percent, is as follows:

(a)   Calculate and sum the present value, discounted at 8 percent, of each of the inflows.

$$\frac{\$500 \text{ (in 3 years)}}{1.08^3} = \frac{\$500}{1.2597} = \$\ 396.92$$

$$\frac{\$1,000 \text{ (in 4 years)}}{1.08^4} = \frac{\$1,000}{1.3605} = 735.02$$

$$\frac{\$2,000 \text{ (in 5 years)}}{1.08^5} = \frac{\$2,000}{1.4693} = 1,361.19$$

$$\frac{\$2,000 \text{ (in 6 years)}}{1.08^6} = \frac{\$2,000}{1.5869} = 1,260.32$$

$$\frac{\$3,000 \text{ (in 7 years)}}{1.08^7} = \frac{\$3,000}{1.7138} = \underline{1,750.50}$$

Total $5,503.95

(b)   Calculate and sum the present value, discounted at 8 percent, of each of the outflows.

$$\$2,000 \text{ (in 0 years)} \qquad\qquad = \$2,000.00$$

$$\frac{\$1,000 \text{ (in 1 year)}}{1.08^1} = \frac{\$1,000}{1.08} = 925.93$$

$$\frac{\$500 \text{ (in 2 years)}}{1.08^2} = \frac{\$500}{1.1664} = \underline{428.67}$$

Total $3,354.60

(c)   Subtract the result of step two from that of step one to produce the positive NPV of $2,149.35.

90.   One more complicating factor may be the presence of one or more years in which there is no cash outflow or inflow. This does not change the procedure for solving the problem, but it does require a little extra care to make sure the inflows and outflows are being discounted for the correct number of years. For example, if the last illustration is changed so that there is no cash inflow at the end of years three and four (see the bottom time line in figure 2.4), the NPV on the basis of an 8 percent discount rate would be as follows:

(a)   Present value of inflows

$2,000 (in 5 years)	=	$1,361.19
$2,000 (in 6 years)	=	1,260.32
$3,000 (in 7 years)	=	1,750.50
Total		$4,372.01

(b)   Present value of outflows

$2,000 (in 0 years)	=	$2,000.00
$1,000 (in 1 year)	=	925.93
$500 (in 2 years)	=	428.67
Total		$3,354.60

(c)   Net Present Value $1,017.41

91.   The final bit of complexity to be introduced at this point is the presence of one or more cash outflows after the stream of cash inflows has begun. Any inflows and outflows that occur in the same year should be netted against each other. This may produce either of these results: a net cash inflow that is smaller than it otherwise would have been, a net cash inflow that is zero, or a net cash outflow. The first two results involve no new procedures in finding the NPV. The third result does require a little extra work to compute the NPV. (As you will see later, this type of result may greatly complicate the task of computing an internal rate of return, however.)

92.   Consider, for example, an investment that calls for the following pattern of cash flows (see figure 2.5):

Beginning of Year	Cash Flow
1	$3,000 outflow
2	$2,000 outflow
3	0
4	$1,000 inflow
5	$2,000 outflow
6	$3,000 inflow
7	$3,000 inflow
8	$3,000 inflow

FIGURE 2.5
Time Line Representation of NPV Problem: Series of Outflows Followed by Year of Zero Flow Followed by Series of Inflows Interrupted by Outflow

---

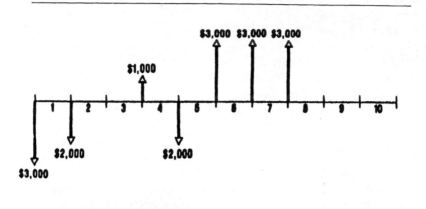

This line shows a series of decreasing cash outflows followed by one year in which there is no net inflow or outflow. Thereafter comes one year of a net cash inflow and one of a net cash outflow. Finally, three years of level net cash inflows occur.

---

93.   In this case, the only new procedure for solving the problem is that you must remember to add to the present value of the initial outflows in years one and two the present value of the outflow that occurs at the beginning of year five. If, for instance, a 7 percent discount rate is assumed, the present values are as shown below.

(a)   Present value of inflows:

$$\$1{,}000 \text{ (in 3 years)} = \frac{\$1{,}000}{1.07^3} = \frac{\$1{,}000}{1.2250} = \$816.33$$

$$\$3{,}000 \text{ (in 5 years)} = \frac{\$3{,}000}{1.07^5} = \frac{\$3{,}000}{1.4026} = 2{,}138.88$$

$$\$3{,}000 \text{ (in 6 years)} = \frac{\$3{,}000}{1.07^6} = \frac{\$3{,}000}{1.5007} = 1{,}999.07$$

$$\$3{,}000 \text{ (in 7 years)} = \frac{\$3{,}000}{1.07^7} = \frac{\$3{,}000}{1.6058} = \underline{1{,}868.23}$$

Total $6,822.51

(b)   Present value of outflows:

$3,000 (in 0 years)   = $3,000.00

$$\$2{,}000 \text{ (in 1 year)} = \frac{\$2{,}000}{1.07} = 1{,}869.16$$

$$\$2{,}000 \text{ (in 4 years)} = \frac{\$2{,}000}{1.07^4} = \frac{\$2{,}000}{1.3108} = \underline{1{,}525.79}$$

Total $6,394.95

(c)   Net present value $ 427.56

                       800-795-5347

94.   In all the net present value illustrative problems up to this point, the solution could be found fairly easily because the pattern of cash flows was short. As was explained earlier, tools such as the time-value formulas and a simple calculator suffice in such situations for computing and totaling the present values of the individual cash flows or, in the case of a series of level cash flows, the annuity.

95.   As net present value problems start to become more involved, however, the use of formulas starts to be cumbersome. Then a calculator like the HP-12C, the HP-10B II, the HP-17B II, or the BA-II Plus, or perhaps even a computer, becomes necessary.

Computing Net Present Value: Complex Problems

Ungrouped Cash Flows

96.   Now we will take up somewhat more complicated problems. First to be explained is the use of the calculators to solve NPV problems in which there are no consecutive cash flows that are of the same amount and sign. To solve an NPV problem on the HP-12C, where the cash flows are ungrouped, the procedure is the same as that explained earlier in this chapter. You will be using the blue CFo and CFj keys in the top row of the keyboard. In addition, you will need to use the CHS key to enter outflows as negative numbers. Also, you will be entering the discount rate using the i key as usual. Finally, you will use the yellow f key and the NPV function to produce the solution. To solve the same type of problem on the HP-10B II, the HP-17B II, or the BA-II Plus, you will again be using the cash flow mode explained earlier in this chapter. In addition, however, you will use the +/- key to enter outflows as negative numbers. You will enter the discount rate into the calculator just as before and use the NPV function to produce the answer.

97.   To illustrate the process, assume that you have been asked to make a $75,000 loan. The borrower agrees to the following repayment schedule:

End of year 1	$ 0
End of year 2	$15,000
End of year 3	$20,000
End of year 4	$25,000
End of year 5	$30,000

If you insist on a rate of return of at least 11 percent on your investment, should you enter into this loan?

98.   On the HP-12C, press 75000, CHS, blue g, and CFo. The initial outlay (at the beginning of the first year) has now been entered as a negative amount. Press 0, blue g, and CFj to reflect the fact that in the first year following the initial outlay, there is no net cash inflow or outflow. Press 15000, blue g, and CFj to enter the positive cash inflow at the end of year two. Enter the remaining three inflows by pressing 20000, blue g, CFj; 25000, blue g, CFj; and 30000, blue g, CFj. Now enter the minimum acceptable rate of return by pressing 11 and the i key. Finally, compute the NPV by pressing the yellow f key and NPV. The answer, –$13,930.02, appears on the display.

99.   On the HP-10B II, press 75000, +/-, CF$_j$. The initial outlay (at the start of the first year) has now been entered as a negative amount. Press 0, CF$_j$, to reflect the fact that at the end of the first year, there is no net cash inflow or outflow. Then enter the remaining cash inflows by pressing 15000, CF$_j$, 20000, CF$_j$, 25000, CF$_j$, 30000, CF$_j$. Now press 11 and I/YR to enter the minimum acceptable rate of return. Then press shift and NPV to produce the answer, –$13,930.02.

100.   On the HP-17B II, enter the CFLO menu system and turn off the #T? function. Then press 75000, +/-, and INPUT. The initial outlay (at the beginning of the first year) has now been entered as a negative amount. Press 0 and INPUT to reflect the fact that in the first year following the initial outlay, there is no net cash inflow or outflow. Press 15000, and INPUT to enter the positive cash inflow at the end of year two. Enter the remaining three inflows by pressing 20000, INPUT, 25000, INPUT, 30000, and INPUT. Now press EXIT and the CALC menu key. Enter the minimum acceptable rate of return by pressing 11 and the I% menu key. Finally, press the NPV menu key to produce the answer, –$13,930.02.

101.   Or, if you use the BA-II Plus, press CF, 2nd, and CLR Work. Then press 75000, +/-, ENTER, and ↓. The initial outlay (at the start of the first year) has now been entered as a negative amount. Press 0, ENTER, ↓, ↓ to reflect the fact that at the end of the first year, there is no net cash inflow or outflow. Then enter each of the remaining cash inflows by pressing 15000, ENTER, ↓, ↓, 20000, ENTER, ↓, ↓, 25000, ENTER, ↓, ↓, 30000, ENTER, ↓, ↓. Now press NPV, 11, ENTER, ↓, and CPT to insert the minimum acceptable rate of return and to produce the solution. The answer, -$13,930.02, appears on the display.

102.   Obviously, this project should be rejected since, in light of the time value of money, it would cost you almost $14,000. This project would be unacceptable even if you were willing to settle for as little as a 5 percent rate of return.

> On the HP-12C, press 5, i, yellow f, and NPV.
> On the HP-10B II, press 5, I/YR, shift, and NPV.
> On the HP-17B II, press 5, the I% menu key, and the NPV menu key.
> On the BA-II Plus press NPV, 5, ENTER, ↓, and CPT.

Note that the net present value even at this rate is a negative $44.46.

Grouped Cash Flows

103 .   These financial calculators can solve NPV problems involving more cash flows if there are grouped data, that is, if some of the consecutive cash flows are of the same sign and are of equal amounts. As was explained earlier in this chapter, for such problems you should enter, along with the amount of each such cash flow, the total number of times it occurs in succession, including the first time.

104.   To illustrate the NPV process, assume that you are considering investing in an oil exploration venture that you believe will entail the following cash flows:

Initial outlay	$50,000
Inflows at end of years 1-5	0
Inflows at end of years 6-9	$ 6,000
Inflow at end of year 10	$60,000

Is this investment acceptable if you insist on a rate of return of at least 12 percent per year?

105.   After clearing the HP-12C, begin by entering the amount of the initial outflow: 50000, CHS, blue g, and CFo. Now enter the first group of inflows by pressing 0, blue g, and CFj. Since this amount will occur a total of five times (including the first), press 5, blue g, and Nj. Now enter the next group of inflows: 6000, blue g, CFj, and the number of times this amount will occur: 4, blue g, Nj. Then enter the last inflow, 60000, blue g, CFj. Finally, enter the required interest rate by pressing 12 and i. Compute the answer by pressing yellow f and NPV, and the answer, –$20,340.76, appears on the screen. Another "great" investment to be avoided!

106.   If you are using the HP-10B II, clear it (Did I need to tell you?) and enter the initial cash outflow by pressing 50000, +/-, and CF_j. Now enter the first group of inflows by pressing 0 and CF_j. Since this amount will occur a total of five times (including the first), press 5, shift, and N_j. Now enter the next group of inflows: 6000, CF_j, and the number of times this amount will occur: 4, shift, and N_j. Then enter the last inflow, 60000 and CF_j. Finally, enter the required interest rate by pressing 12 and I/YR. Compute the answer by pressing shift and NPV. The answer is –$20,340.76. Looks like a good project to stay out of!

107.   If you are using the HP-17B II, enter the CFLO menu system and turn on the #T? function. Now enter the initial outflow by pressing 50000, +/-, and INPUT. Then enter the first group of inflows by pressing 0 and INPUT. Since this will occur a total of five times (including the first), press 5 and INPUT. Now enter the next group of inflows: 6000, INPUT, 4, and INPUT. Then enter the last inflow: 60000, INPUT, 1, and INPUT. Then press EXIT, the CALC menu key, 12, and the I% menu key. Press the NPV menu key to produce the answer, –$20,340.76. This is a "great" investment that you definitely don't need!

108.   Or, if you are using the BA-II Plus, enter the cash flow prompted worksheet and clear it of extraneous data. (You didn't have to be reminded, did you?) Then press the following keys:

50000, +/-, ENTER, ↓, 0, ENTER, ↓, 5, ENTER, ↓,
6000, ENTER, ↓, 4, ENTER, ↓, 60000, ENTER, ↓, 1,
ENTER, ↓, NPV, 12, ENTER, ↓, CPT

The answer, –$20,340.76, appears on the screen. A "great" investment that you can get along without!

Computing Internal Rate of Return

109.   Recall the definition of the second technique for discounted cash flow analysis. The internal rate of return generated by an investment is the interest rate that equates the present value of the cash inflows and outflows, producing a net present value of zero. If the IRR exceeds the investor's minimum required rate of return, the investment is an attractive one. If it equals the minimum required rate, the investor should be neutral toward the project. If the IRR is below the minimum required rate, the investment is unattractive.

110.   The mathematics of computing the IRR of an investment are extremely complex. The process is essentially one of trial and error. To solve the problem manually, you must begin with an estimate of what the IRR might be.[6] Some authors suggest that a rate such as 10 percent or 15 percent is usually a reasonable starting point. The cash inflows and outflows are then discounted to their present values using that rate and compared. If the present value of the inflows exceeds the present value of the outflows (that is, if there is a positive NPV at that rate), the rate being used is below the actual IRR, so you must select a higher rate and repeat the calculations. (Remember that present values move in a direction opposite that of interest rates. Here, you are looking for a smaller net present value, namely, zero, so you must increase the interest rate being used.) On the other hand, if with a given interest rate the discounted cash outflows exceed the discounted cash inflows (that is, if there is a negative NPV), you must select a lower interest rate and repeat the calculations. Continue this trial-and-error process, using higher and lower interest rates to discount the cash flows, until the resulting NPV is equal to or very close to zero. The rate producing this result is the IRR, which is an average rate of return over the period under consideration, weighted to reflect the amount and timing of the various cash flows.

111.   Given the complexity and time needed to solve even simple IRR problems manually, use of a financial calculator to do so is much more practical. The procedure for solving IRR problems with financial calculators is very similar to that for NPV problems. The only differences in the procedure are as follows:

(a)   When solving for IRR, you do not enter a discount rate since this is what you are trying to find. Therefore, skip the next to last portion of the NPV sequence.

(b)   On the HP-12C, instead of pressing yellow f and the NPV function after all the data have been entered, press yellow f and the IRR function, which is located on the FV key.

(c)   On the HP-10B II, instead of pressing shift and NPV after all the data have been entered, press shift and IRR/YR, which is on the key to the left of NPV.

(d)   On the HP-17B II, instead of pressing the NPV menu key after all the data have been entered, press the IRR% menu key, which is immediately to the left of the I% menu key.

(e)   On the BA-II Plus, instead of pressing NPV, the discount rate, ENTER, ↓, and CPT after all the cash flows have been entered, simply press IRR in the second row of the keyboard and CPT.

112.   For example, to solve an earlier illustrative problem (a single outflow of $10,000 followed by five inflows of $2,739.80 each), set the calculator to display four decimal places.

113.   Then on the HP-12C press the following keys: 10000, CHS, blue g, CFo, 2739.80, blue g, CFj, 5, blue g, Nj, yellow f, and IRR.

114.   Or, on the HP-10B II, press 10000, +/-, CF_j, 2,739.80, CF_j, 5, shift, N_j, shift, and IRR/YR.

115.   Or, on the HP-17B II, turn the #T? function on and press 10000, +/-, INPUT, 2739.80, INPUT, 5, INPUT, EXIT, the CALC menu key, and the IRR% menu key.

116.   Or, on the BA-II Plus press 10000, +/-, ENTER, ↓, 2739.80, ENTER, ↓, 5, ENTER, ↓, IRR, and CPT.

117.   You may have to wait for a few seconds for the answer to appear because of the complex mathematical characteristics of the IRR calculation. The answer, 11.4997 percent, will be displayed on the screen.

118.   Or, to take a more involved example, assume that an investment you are considering involves a $60,000 initial outlay and then the following series of cash flows:

End of Year	Cash Flow	End of Year	Cash Flow
1	$2,000 inflow	6	$10,000 outflow
2	$9,000 inflow	7	$11,000 inflow
3	$9,000 inflow	8	0
4	$9,000 inflow	9	$12,000 inflow
5	$9,000 inflow	10	$30,000 inflow

119.   The keystrokes on the HP-12C are as follows:

Initial outlay	60000, CHS, blue g, CFo
Year 1	2000, blue g, CFj
Years 2-5	9000, blue g, CFj, 4, blue g, Nj
Year 6	10000, CHS, blue g, CFj
Year 7	11000, blue g, CFj
Year 8	0, blue g, CFj
Year 9	12000, blue g, CFj
Year 10	30000, blue g, CFj

Then press the yellow f key and IRR. After this relatively slow machine runs through the trial-and-error process for several seconds, the answer, 4.6664 percent, will be displayed.

120.   The keystrokes on the HP-10B II are as follows:

Initial outlay	60000, +/-, CF$_j$
Year 1	2000, CF$_j$
Years 2-5	9000, CF$_J$ 4, shift, N$_j$
Year 6	10000, +/-, CF$_j$
Year 7	11000, CF$_j$

Year 8	0, CF$_j$
Year 9	12000, CF$_j$
Year 10	30000, CF$_j$

Then press shift and IRR/YR to produce the answer, 4.6664 percent.

121.   The keystrokes on the HP-17B II, with the #T? function turned on, would be as follows:

Initial outlay	60000, +/-, INPUT
Year 1	2000, INPUT, 1, INPUT
Years 2-5	9000, INPUT, 4, INPUT
Year 6	10000, +/-, INPUT, 1, INPUT
Year 7	11000, INPUT, 1, INPUT
Year 8	0, INPUT, 1, INPUT
Year 9	12000, INPUT, 1, INPUT
Year 10	30000, INPUT, 1, INPUT

Then press EXIT, the CALC menu key, and the IRR% menu key.   The answer will be displayed very quickly as 4.6664%.

122.   The keystrokes on the BA-II Plus would be as follows:

Initial outlay	60000, +/-, ENTER, ↓
Year 1	2000, ENTER, ↓, ↓
Years 2-5	9000, ENTER, ↓, 4, ENTER, ↓
Year 6	10000, +/-, ENTER, ↓, ↓
Year 7	11000, ENTER, ↓, ↓
Year 8	0, ENTER, ↓, ↓
Year 9	12000, ENTER, ↓, ↓
Year 10	30000, ENTER, ↓

Then press IRR and CPT. After a few seconds, the answer, 4.6664 percent, will be displayed.

Problems in Decision Making Based on IRR

123.   The internal rate of return as a measure of the desirability of a proposed investment is more familiar to most decision makers than net present value. However, IRR must be used with caution as the basis for *ranking* alternative investment opportunities, especially if they are *mutually exclusive*. In such

situations, choices based solely on IRRs may not be the wisest ones.

124.   One situation in which an evaluation based solely on comparative IRRs may lead to an incorrect decision is the case of mutually exclusive investment projects that are of substantially different magnitudes. Assume, for example, that you can invest in either of two pieces of equipment for your business, but that investment in one would eliminate the possibility or need for investing in the other for some technical reason. Assume also that you have or can borrow enough money so that you are free to invest in either type of equipment. The total cash flows from the two projects, A and B, are as shown below, and neither piece of equipment will have any salvage value.

Beginning of Year	Cash Flow (A)	Cash Flow (B)
1	$5,000 outflow	$50,000 outflow
2	$3,000 inflow	$25,000 inflow
3	$4,000 inflow	$35,000 inflow
4	$5,000 inflow	$45,000 inflow

125.   The IRR from project A is 54.0603 percent, while that from project B is only 42.9811 percent. Does this mean that project A is preferable? Not necessarily. For example, if the money to meet the initial outflow is to be borrowed at a 10 percent rate of interest, it may be preferable to invest in project B. On the basis of a 10 percent discount rate, the NPV of project B is $35,462.06, whereas that of project A is only $4,789.63. In other words, project B would increase your wealth (in a time-value sense) by more than seven times the increase that project A would provide. A more modest rate of return on a large project may be preferable to a higher rate of return on a small project. (Note, however, that this illustration deals with *mutually exclusive* projects. In other types of cases, the wise decision might be to invest in both projects.)

126.   A second type of situation in which a decision based solely on IRR may be incorrect is that in which mutually exclusive potential investment projects entail substantially different cash flow patterns. Assume that two competing investment opportunities, C and D, are expected to produce the

total cash flows shown below. Assume also that the two projects are mutually exclusive because you are able to borrow only $30,000, the amount of the initial cash outlay for each. The interest rate the lender will charge and, therefore, the discount rate you have decided to use in evaluating the two projects is 12 percent per year.

Beginning of Year	Cash Flow (C)	Cash Flow (D)
1	$30,000 outflow	$30,000 outflow
2-5	$11,000 inflow	$ 5,000 inflow
6-20	0	$ 5,000 inflow

127.   The IRR from project C is 17.2968 percent, while that from project D is only 15.6071 percent. The NPV of project D, however, is $6,828.88 at a discount rate of 12 percent, whereas it is only $3,410.84 for project C. Once again, the project with the lower IRR provides a greater addition to your wealth (in a time-value sense).

128.   If all of that isn't sufficiently confusing, you should recognize that the discount rate that is used may affect the ranking of the two projects on the basis of the NPVs. Projects in which a large percentage of the cash inflows occur late have NPVs that are significantly affected by a change in the discount rate. This is the case with project D. Projects in which a large percentage of the cash inflows occur early, like project C, have NPVs that are less affected by a change in the discount rate. Consequently, a "back-end loaded" project may have a better NPV at a low discount rate than a "front-end loaded" project, but a worse NPV at a high discount rate. For example, calculate the NPV of projects C and D at a 19 percent discount rate. Under that assumption, project C has both the better IRR and the better (actually, the less bad) NPV.[7]

129.   There is also a difficulty in relying solely on IRRs when deciding between mutually exclusive investment opportunities that have substantially different durations. The IRR method includes no explicit assumption about the rate of return at which funds released from a short-duration project will be able to be reinvested. In the preceding example, project D will generate an annual IRR of over 15 percent for 20 years. Project C provides an annual IRR of a bit over 17 percent, but for only five years.

Assume that the rates of return available on investments of comparable risk fall substantially during the next few years. This means that the heavy early cash inflows from project C will have to be reinvested at rates so unattractive that the combined IRR from project C and its successor(s) over the full 20 years will be less than its five-year IRR, and perhaps even less than the 20-year IRR of project D.

130.   Still another limitation of the IRR method for comparing mutually exclusive investment projects is similar to the last one but involves a question of the cost of financing cash outflows that may be associated with one or both of the projects. Consider the following set of cash flows from investment projects E and F.

Beginning of Year	Cash Flow (E)	Cash Flow (F)
1	$10,000 outflow	$10,000 outflow
2	$ 1,000 inflow	0
3	$ 5,000 outflow	0
4	$ 5,000 inflow	0
5	$ 5,000 inflow	0
6	$ 5,000 inflow	$ 3,000 inflow
7	$ 5,000 inflow	$13,000 inflow

On the surface, project E appears to be clearly preferable. Its IRR appears to be (more on that below) 9.7283 percent versus 8.4315 percent for project F. And, if a reasonable discount rate is used, such as 8 percent, for calculating NPV, project E wins again, $837.31 versus $233.95.

131.   But, notice that project E requires a $5,000 cash outflow at the beginning of year three. Presumably, that amount will have to be borrowed at some rate of interest or taken out of some other investment where it is earning some rate of return. In either case, there is a cost to the investor, either a direct cost or an opportunity cost, arising from the need to cover the cash outflow. If interest rates should rise substantially during the first two years of the project, that cost alone might be sufficient to drive the actual IRR of project E below that of project F.

132.   A final problem to be discussed here concerning the IRR method is that it is possible for a project to have more than one

IRR, each of which is mathematically correct. It is also possible that an investment may have no IRR. A mathematical explanation of how these results can be produced is beyond the scope of this book. They can arise, however, whenever the stream of outflows and inflows involves more than one change of sign between negative and positive (for example, one or more outflows followed by one or more inflows followed by one or more outflows, as was the case in connection with project E-above).

133.   How can you tell whether an investment might have more than one internal rate of return? Look over the pattern of net cash outflows and inflows.   Often, there will be only one change of sign in these net flows over the lifetime of the investment. The sequence might begin with one or a few periods of net cash outflows (minus signs) followed by a series of net cash inflows (plus signs), perhaps with an occasional net inflow of zero (still a plus sign), until the project is concluded. Where there is only one sign change, there is only one internal rate of return. If there is more than one sign change, however, there *may* be more than one IRR, or there may be no IRR at all. All of the answers will be mathematically correct – and none of them will be of much help as a basis for making an intelligent decision.[8]

134.   If you are using the HP-12C, HP-10B II, HP-17B II, or BA-II Plus to compute the IRR of an investment, the calculator will usually let you know if it is having trouble computing the one-and-only correct internal rate of return and will display an error message.

135.   What do you do about all these problems in using IRR as a basis for deciding about a very complicated investment? One simple solution is to "punt." Perhaps you should forget about trying to use IRR as a method of evaluating the particular investment. Rather, use the NPV method. Another approach is to use one of several *modified* IRR methods that have been developed. One of these is described below.

Modified Internal Rate of Return (MIRR)

136.   A modified internal rate of return calculation entails: (a) reducing a series of cash flows having multiple sign changes to one that has only one sign change, and (b) specifying the

reinvestment rate that will apply, rather than assuming that the project's IRR will be the applicable reinvestment rate. In these ways, MIRR may be superior to IRR, while still expressing the solution as the familiar yield or rate of return that decision makers sometimes prefer to the fuzzy notion of NPV.

137.   The first step in computing a project's MIRR is to select a rate, usually a conservative (low) one, at which it is safe to assume that the project's cash inflows can be reinvested until the end of the project. The second step is to compute the future value (sometimes called the *terminal value*) of all those inflows as of the end of the project's life. The third step is to discount (find the present value of) all the project's outflows back to the origination point of the project. The final step is to compute the annual rate of return represented by the difference between the present value of the outflows and the future or terminal value of the inflows over the life of the project.

138.   To illustrate, assume that a proposed investment is likely to entail the following series of cash flows:

Initial outlay	$1,500,000
Inflow at end of year 1	125,000
Outflow at end of year 2	150,000
Inflow at end of year 3	0
Inflow at end of year 4	200,000
Inflow at end of year 5	1,900,000

If a safe reinvestment rate of 5 percent is assumed, what is this investment's MIRR?

(a)   The future or terminal value of the inflows at 5 percent is $125,000 for four years, plus $200,000 for one year, plus $1,900,000, or a total of $2,261,938.28.

(b)   The present value of the outflows at 5 percent is $1,500,000, plus $150,000 for two years, or a total of $1,636,054.42.

(c)   The life of the project is five years.

(d)   In the calculator, insert $2,261,938.28 as the FV, $1,636,054.42 as the negative PV, and 5 as the number of periods. Solve for the interest rate, which is 6.6932%. This is the modified IRR based on an assumed 5 percent reinvestment rate.

139.   The use of MIRR doesn't solve all the problems that arise when comparing mutually exclusive projects. For example, an investment with a high MIRR and a low NPV might be less desirable than one with a lower MIRR and a higher NPV. Therefore, NPV is still the most reliable tool for ranking competing investments. MIRR is often, however, an improvement over IRR in such circumstances.

INCREASING THE COMPOUNDING, DISCOUNTING, OR PAYMENT FREQUENCY

140.   All the explanations and illustrations so far in this and the preceding chapter have been based on the assumption that compounding and discounting to determine the time value of money occur once per year. In reality, however, compounding and discounting often occur more frequently than annually. For example, a certificate of deposit may be credited with compound interest on a monthly basis. A NOW account may earn daily compound interest. The yield or the present value of the income from a corporate bond typically is computed on the basis of semiannual discounting.

141.   In addition, all of the explanations of problems involving periodic payments thus far have been based on the assumption that the payments are made annually. Often, however, such payments occur more than once per year. Installment loan payments, for example, often are made monthly. Bond interest payments usually are made every six months. Deposits into the savings accounts of many people are made biweekly.

142.   The remainder of this chapter examines the effect on the interest rate and, therefore, on the time value of money resulting from compounding or discounting more often than annually. This chapter also contains an explanation of how to solve problems involving a series of level payments that occur more often than once per year, regardless of how often per year compounding or discounting takes place.

Nominal Versus Effective Interest Rates

143.   As you know, compounding results in the conversion of interest earnings into principal. For example, if $100 is deposited today and subsequently is credited with $7.00 of compound interest, the principal on which future interest will be credited rises to $107. The $7.00 of interest becomes converted into principal.

144.   If compounding occurs annually, when does interest become converted into principal and begin to earn interest on itself? Obviously, the conversion and thus the capacity for increased interest earnings occur after one year, again after two years, and so on. If, on the other hand, compounding occurs on, for example, a monthly basis, when does interest become converted to principal and thus begin to earn interest on itself? The conversions occur after one month has elapsed, again after two months, three months, etc.

145.   Of course, the greater the frequency with which compounding occurs, the smaller will be the dollar amount of interest earned and converted into principal on the occasion of each compounding. Naturally, the amount of interest a given amount of principal can earn in a week, for example, is less than it can earn in a month at any given stated or nominal annual interest rate. Nevertheless, all other things being equal, the more frequently compounding occurs per year, the greater will be the *total* amount of interest credited to an account in the year. To illustrate, table 2.2 shows the amount of interest that will be credited during one year to a $5,000 deposit with a stated or nominal 9 percent annual interest rate if that 9 percent rate is applied with various frequencies during the year.

146.   Technically, of course, compounding can occur even more frequently than daily - every hour, every minute, every second, or even more frequently than that. And, as the frequency continues to increase, so does the total interest credited. The upper limit of the total interest credited to a sum of money for a particular stated or nominal annual interest rate occurs in the case of continuous compounding, wherein interest is compounded an infinite number of times per year, rather than at discrete time intervals. Continuous compounding is a theoretical concept, useful principally in the study of advanced financial topics, but it also has some practical applications since financial

institutions occasionally credit interest to customer accounts on a continuous basis.

TABLE 2.2

Total Interest Credited to a $5,000 Deposit During One Year at 9% Stated Annual Interest Rate and Various Compounding Frequencies

---

Compounding Frequency	Interest Earnings
Annually	$450.00
Semiannually	460.13
Quarterly	465.42
Monthly	469.03
Weekly	470.45
Daily*	470.81

*Based on 360 days per year.[9]

---

147.   From the figures in table 2.2, it should be obvious that a stated or nominal annual interest rate does not necessarily reflect the true or effective interest rate. You have seen that a 9 percent nominal annual rate produces any of six separate interest earnings in a year, depending on the frequency with which compounding occurs. Hence, it is important to distinguish between the nominal or stated annual rate (9 percent in this illustration) and the true or effective annual rate.

148.   When compounding occurs once per year, the nominal and effective annual rates are identical. In table 2.2, the $5,000 deposit earned $450, exactly 9 percent, when annual compounding was applied. In all other cases, it earned more than $450, more than 9 percent, because compounding occurred more than once per year.

149.   The effective annual interest rate is defined as the annual rate that would produce in one compounding the same amount of interest as does the nominal annual rate with its compounding frequency. For instance, the 9 percent nominal annual rate in table 2.2, when compounded quarterly, produced $465.42 of interest. Thus, the effective annual interest rate was ($465.42 ÷ $5,000 =) 9.3084 percent. Similarly, the 9 percent nominal annual rate compounded daily generated $470.81 of interest. Thus, the effective annual rate was ($470.81 ÷ $5,000 =) 9.4162 percent.

Calculating the Effective Annual Rate

150.   The effective annual interest rate can be computed for any nominal rate and compounding frequency by the following formula:[10]

$$i_{eff} = \left[1 + \frac{i_{nom}}{f} \right]^f - 1$$

Where: i_{eff} is the effective annual rate

i_{nom} is the nominal annual rate

f is the compounding frequency per year

Thus, for example, a 9 percent nominal annual rate compounded monthly represents an effective annual rate of:

$$\left[1 + \frac{.09}{12} \right]^{12} - 1$$

$$= \qquad 9.3807\%$$

151.   As an alternative to using this formula, you can calculate the effective interest rate for any nominal annual rate and compounding frequency by using the HP-12C, HP-10B II, HP-17B II, or BA-II Plus calculator. To illustrate, assume that a 7 percent nominal rate is to be compounded weekly.

152. Set the HP-12C calculator to display four decimal places. Then press the following keys:

7, ENTER,	(to enter the nominal rate)
52, ÷, i,	(to enter the weekly
52, n	frequency of
	compounding)
100, CHS, ENTER,	(to produce the effective
PV, FV, +	rate)

The answer, 7.2458 percent, appears on the display.

153. Or, set the HP-10B II to display four decimal places. Then, in order to convert a nominal rate to an effective rate, you will need to use the functions printed on the I/YR, PV, and PMT keys. For the problem at hand, press:

7, shift, NOM%	(to enter the nominal rate)
52, shift, P/YR	(to enter the weekly frequency of compounding)
shift, EFF%	(to produce the effective rate)

The effective rate is 7.2458 percent. Now before you do anything else, restore the calculator's setting to one payment period and one compounding period per year. Otherwise, subsequent problems you work on will be solved incorrectly. Press 1, shift, P/YR, shift, and C.

154. If you are using the HP-17B II, set it to display four decimal places. Then enter the interest rate conversion menu system by pressing the ICNV menu key, which is next to the TVM menu key. Then press the PER menu key since in this and almost all problems, compounding is periodic, rather than continuous. Then press 7 and the NOM% menu key to enter the nominal rate, 52 and the P menu key to enter the weekly frequency of compounding, and the EFF% menu key to produce the effective annual rate, 7.2458 percent.

155. If you use the BA-II Plus, set the calculator to display four decimal places. Then press 2nd and IConv (for interest rate conversion), which is located on the number 2 key. Then press 7, ENTER, ↓, ↓ (to put the nominal rate into the machine), 52, ENTER, ↑ (to put the number of compounding periods per year

into the machine), and CPT. The answer, 7.2458 percent, appears on the display.

156.   For those who do not wish to use either a formula or a financial calculator to determine the effective interest rate, Appendix E at the end of this book will be of some help. It contains a table showing the effective annual interest rate that corresponds to a number of nominal annual rates and commonly used compounding frequencies. The table also includes the effective rate for the unusual case of continuous compounding.

157.   To illustrate further the difference between the nominal and effective annual rates of interest, the following list shows the effective rate for a nominal rate of 7 percent with various compounding frequencies.

7% annually	=	7.0000% effective rate
7% semiannually	=	7.1225% effective rate
7% quarterly	=	7.1859% effective rate
7% monthly	=	7.2290% effective rate
7% weekly	=	7.2458% effective rate
7% daily (360)	=	7.2501% effective rate

158.   Again, it is clear that for a particular nominal annual interest rate, the true or effective rate rises as the frequency of compounding per year increases. Note, however, that the increase in the effective rate becomes smaller and smaller with each increase in compounding frequency. In the above list, for example, the change from annual to semiannual compounding increased the effective rate by (7.1225 – 7.0000 =) .1225 percentage points. The change from semiannual to quarterly compounding changed the effective rate by only (7.1859 – 7.1225 =) .0634 percentage points, and the change from quarterly to monthly compounding increased it by only (7.2290 – 7.1859 =) .0431 percentage points.

159.   Another point worth noting concerning nominal versus effective annual interest rates is that sometimes a low nominal rate with a high compounding frequency will produce a higher effective rate than a high nominal rate with a low compounding frequency. For example, assume that you plan to deposit $10,000 in an interest-bearing account for one year. Bank A pays interest of 8 percent compounded semiannually. Bank B pays 7.9 percent compounded daily (360 days per year). Where

should you put your money? If you were to use the formula described earlier or a financial calculator, you would find that the effective rate in Bank A is 8.1600 percent. Bank B, on the other hand, pays an effective rate of 8.2195 percent. That is an extra $5.95 that will be credited to your $10,000 deposit if you go to Bank B.

Impact of Compounding Frequency on Future Values

160.   Because the effective interest rate rises as the frequency of compounding of a particular nominal annual interest rate increases, so does the future value of a single sum. The same is true of other future values described in this and the previous chapter. For example, the future value of an annual annuity or of a series of annual uneven cash flows rises as compounding frequency increases. Conversely, in sinking fund problems, the size of the annual payment needed to reach a targeted future amount diminishes as the frequency of compounding and the effective interest rate increase. Finally, the number of years or of annual payments needed to reach a particular future value decreases as the frequency of compounding and the effective interest rate increase.

Impact of Discounting Frequency on Present Values

161.   You probably have already guessed that increasing the frequency of discounting has the opposite effect on present values from the effect that increasing the frequency of compounding has on future values. This again follows from the preceding discussion of nominal versus effective interest rates.

162.   To illustrate, calculate the present value of $100 due in one year at 7 percent. Discounted annually, you know that the effective rate is 7 percent. The present value of $100 for one year at 7 percent is $93.46. Discounted quarterly, however, the effective rate is 7.1859 percent. The present value of $100 for one year at 7.1859 percent is $93.30. And, discounted monthly, the effective rate is 7.2290 percent, which produces a present value of $93.26. Generalizing from these results, then, you can conclude that, all other things being equal, an increase in the frequency with which discounting occurs increases the effective interest rate and, therefore, reduces the present value of a single sum. The same is true of the present value of an annual annuity or of a series of annual uneven cash flows. Conversely, in debt

service problems, an increase in the frequency of charging interest per year, all other things being equal, increases the amount of the loan payments per year. Finally, the number of years it will take to pay off a loan or to liquidate a principal sum increases as the frequency of charging or crediting interest per year increases, all other things being equal.

Calculating Future and Present Values

163.   When you encounter a time-value-of-money problem in which the interest rate is compounded or discounted more than once per year, there are two basic ways of solving it: using the effective rate or adjusting the nominal rate and number of periods.

Using the Effective Rate

164.   The first basic approach is to begin solving the problem by computing the effective interest rate, as explained earlier. Then use the effective rate in the same way as you have learned to use the nominal annual interest rate throughout this and the preceding chapter.

165.   For example, to what amount will $500 grow in three years at 6 percent compounded quarterly? The effective rate is 6.1364 percent. Therefore, you can use this rate in place of 6 percent in the FVSS formula. Specifically:

$$FVSS = \$500 \, (1.061364)^3$$

$$= \$500 \times 1.1956$$

$$= \$597.80$$

166.   Or, what is the present value of a five-year annuity of $2,000 if it is discounted at 8 percent weekly? The effective rate is 8.3220 percent. Therefore, you can use this rate in place of 8 percent in the PVA formula. Specifically:

$$PVA = \frac{\left[1 - \dfrac{1}{(1.083220)^5}\right]}{.083220} \times \$2,000$$

$$= \frac{\left[1 - \dfrac{1}{1.4914}\right]}{.083220} \times \$2,000$$

$$= \frac{1 - .6705}{.083220} \times \$2,000$$

$$= 3.9594 \times \$2,000$$

$$= \$7,918.80$$

167.   Instead of using a formula, you can solve these problems by means of your financial calculator. Again, however, you should first calculate the effective rate. Then, follow the normal series of keystrokes for the particular type of problem, but insert the effective rate, rather than the nominal rate, into the calculator as the interest rate.

Adjusting the Nominal Rate and Number of Periods

168.   The second basic way of solving these kinds of problems involves using the nominal annual rate, rather than the effective rate. In this case, however, two adjustments must be made. First, the nominal annual interest rate in the problem must be *divided* by the number of compounding or discounting periods per year. The resulting *periodic* interest rate reflects the fact that only a fraction of the annual rate will be applied each time compounding or discounting occurs during the year. Second, the number of years in the problem must be *multiplied* by the number of compounding or discounting periods per year. The resulting number of *periods* reflects the total number of times during the period covered by the problem that compounding or discounting of the fractional annual rate will occur. Note, then, that if this approach is used, the number that is divided into i and the number that is multiplied by n are always the same (four for quarterly compounding or discounting, 12 for monthly, 360 for daily compounding or discounting, etc.).

169.　To illustrate this approach to solving time-value problems, compute the FVSS of $100 at 8 percent compounded quarterly for 20 years. Instead of the usual formula:

$$FVSS = \$100 \, (1.08)^{20} = \$466.10$$

The formula becomes:

$$FVSS = \$100 \, (1.02)^{80} = \$487.54$$

That is, in quarterly compounding, the 8 percent annual rate is divided by four, and the 20-year period is multiplied by four.

170.　Or, if you wish to calculate by means of the formula the present value of $3,000 due six years hence with a discount rate of 12 percent applied monthly, the usual formula:

$$PVSS = \$3,000 \left[\frac{1}{(1.12)^6} \right] = \$1,519.89$$

Is replaced by:

$$PVSS = \$3,000 \left[\frac{1}{(1.01)^{72}} \right] = \$1,465.49$$

That is, in monthly calculating, the 12 percent annual rate is divided by 12, and the 6-year period is multiplied by 12.

171.　Assume that instead of formulas, you wish to use a financial calculator. The only new procedure for problems involving compounding more often than annually is to make the two adjustments referred to above: divide the nominal annual interest rate by the compounding frequency and multiply the number of years by the compounding frequency. These adjustments may by made mentally before data are entered, or they may be made on the calculator itself as part of the data entry process. The latter approach will be illustrated here because the numbers to be used will be a bit too complex to compute mentally.

172.   For example, you might want to know the amount to which $15,000 will grow in four years at an 8 percent nominal annual interest rate if compounding occurs on a weekly basis. The solution process entails entering the initial sum as a present value, entering four years of weekly compounding as the number of periods, and entering 1/52 of 8 percent as the weekly interest rate.

Using the HP-12C

173.   The sequence of keystrokes for solving this problem on the HP-12C is as follows:

15000, CHS, PV	(to enter the initial deposit)
4, ENTER, 52, x, n	(to enter the number of compounding periods)
8, ENTER, 52, ÷, i	(to enter the weekly interest rate)
FV	(to produce the solution)

The answer, $20,651.84, is displayed.

174.   The HP-12C has one additional feature that is a useful shortcut when solving problems involving monthly compounding (or discounting). Note that the n key also has a blue 12x function, and the i key has a blue 12÷ function. These serve to automatically adjust n and i to a monthly basis.

175.   To illustrate, assume that you wish to calculate the payment amount at the end of each month on a $9,000, four-year automobile loan carrying a nominal annual interest rate of 8.8 percent compounded monthly. Press the following keys:

blue g, END	(to set the payment mode to the end of the month)
9000, CHS, PV	(to enter the loan amount)
8.8, blue g, i	(to enter the monthly interest rate)
4, blue g, n	(to enter the number of payments)
PMT	(to produce the solution)

The answer, $223.11, appears on the display.

Using the HP-10B II

176.   If you are using the HP-10B II, you may recall that in Chapter One, para. 54, you were instructed to set the machine for one payment period and one compounding period per year, and not to change that setting. But, now we are dealing with problems involving payments and compounding that occur more than once per year. Should the calculator setting be changed? We strongly recommend against that. Our experience has been that students often forget to return the setting to once per year/once per year, and they forget to check the setting before solving a new problem, so they obtain incorrect answers. Therefore, we repeat: set it for once per year and don't change it!

177.   How, then, does one deal with payments and compounding that occur more frequently than annually? The answer is to enter the number of periods, not the number of years, as the value of N, and the periodic interest rate, not the annual rate, as the value of I/YR. For example, to find the future value of $15,000 in four years at 8 percent compounded weekly, press

15000, +/-, PV	(to enter the initial payment)
4, x, 52, =, N	(to enter the number of compounding periods)
8, ÷, 52, =, I/YR	(to enter the weekly interest rate)
FV	(to produce the solution)

The answer, $20,651.84, is displayed.

Using the HP-17B II

178.   Users of the HP-17B II will recall from Chapter One, para. 62, that they were instructed to set the calculator for one payment per year and one compounding period per year and not to change this setting – ever! But, now we are dealing with payments that occur and compounding that takes place more than once per year. Should the calculator setting be changed? Though doing so will produce a correct answer, we recommend strongly against it. Our experience has been that users of the calculator often forget to change the settings back to once per year/once per year after solving a problem, and they forget to check these settings for accuracy the next time they try solving a

problem, with the result that solutions to subsequent problems are wildly incorrect. Therefore, we prefer to set the calculator for one payment per year and one compounding period per year and not to change that setting – ever!

179.   How, then, does one deal with payments and compounding that occur more frequently than annually?   The answer is to enter the number periods, not the number of years, as the value of N, and the periodic interest rate, not the nominal annual rate, as the value of I%YR.   For example, to find the future value of $15,000 in four years at 8 percent compounded weekly, the keystrokes on the HP-17B in the TVM menu system are as follows:

15000, +/-, the PV menu key	(to enter the initial deposit)
4, x, 52, =, the N menu key	(to enter the number of compounding periods)
8, ÷, 52, =, the I%YR menu key	(to enter the weekly interest rate)
the FV menu key	(to produce the solution)

The answer, $20,651.84, is displayed.

Using the BA-II Plus

180.   Those who are using the BA-II Plus calculator will recall from Chapter One, para. 71, that they were instructed to set the calculator for one payment per year and one compounding period per year and not to change this setting – ever! But, now we are dealing with payments that occur and compounding that takes place more than once per year.   Should the calculator setting be changed?   Though doing so will produce a correct answer, we recommend strongly against it.   Our experience has been that users of the calculator often forget to change the settings back to once per year/once per year after solving a problem, and they forget to check these settings for accuracy the next time they try solving a problem, with the result that solutions to subsequent problems are wildly incorrect. Therefore, we prefer to set the calculator for one payment per year and one compounding period per year and not to change that setting – ever!

181.   How, then, does one deal with payments and compounding that occur more frequently than annually? The answer is to enter the number periods, not the number of years, as the value of N, and the periodic interest rate, not the nominal annual rate, as the value of I/Y. For example, to find the future value of $15,000 in four years at 8 percent compounded weekly, press the following keys:

15000, +/-, PV	(to enter the initial deposit)
4, x, 52, =, N	(to enter the number of compounding periods)
8, ÷, 52, =, I/Y	(to enter the weekly interest rate)
CPT, FV	(to produce the solution)

The answer, $20,651.84, appears on the display screen.

Interpreting the Results of the Calculations

182.   When the solution to a time-value-of-money problem is a value for n, N, or PMT, remember that these are *periodic* values. Therefore, if the frequency is other-than-annual, such as monthly, the solution also is an other-than-annual value, namely, monthly in this case. To convert the solution to an annual basis, therefore, it must be adjusted by, in the case of monthly results, a factor of 12. For example, if a monthly payment is $800, the amount paid per year is ($800 x 12 =) $9,600. Similarly, if the number of monthly payments is 24, the number of years during which payments will be made is (24 ÷ 12 =) 2.

183.   Also, if the solution to a time-value-of-money problem is a value for i, I/YR, I%YR, or I/Y, it, too, is a *periodic* value. If its frequency is other-than-annual, such as monthly, it too should be converted to an annual basis. However, it is insufficient to merely multiply the periodic interest rate value by, in this case, 12 since the result of such a multiplication would be a *nominal* annual rate (often called the APR, or annual percentage rate, by financial institutions). A more accurate result is found by then converting that nominal annual rate to an effective annual rate as described earlier.

184.   For example, assume that you wish to compute the annual interest rate on a $1,000 loan that calls for 12 monthly payments of $99, beginning one month from the date of the

loan. When you enter the data into your calculator, you will initially find as the solution a rate of 2.7553 percent. This, however, is a monthly rate. Multiply it by 12 to find the nominal annual rate, or APR, 33.0631 percent. Then convert this to an effective annual rate as explained earlier. The effective annual rate on this loan is 38.5634 percent.

Annuity Payments Occurring Other Than Annually

185.   Thus far, we have examined problems in which compounding or discounting occurs more frequently than once per year. A related but separate topic is the question of annuity payments that occur more frequently than once per year. (Uneven cash flows that occur other than annually are not dealt with in this book.)

Simple Annuities and Simple Annuities Due

186.   A simple annuity or annuity due is one in which the frequency of payments and the frequency of compounding or discounting are identical. For example, a series of six quarterly deposits that are credited with interest quarterly and that begin three months from now is a simple annuity. Likewise, a series of 15 monthly payments that are discounted on a monthly basis and that begin immediately is a simple annuity due. All of the annuity topics discussed so far in this book have involved simple annuities or simple annuities due because both the payment frequency and the compounding or discounting frequency were identical.

187.   The calculation of the present or future value of a simple annuity or a simple annuity due when payments are more frequent than annual involves the same tools as you have already learned. The same formulas you used for computing FVA, FVAD, PVA, and PVAD can be used; the same keystrokes can be used on the HP-12C, HP-10B II, HP-17B II, or BA-II Plus – *except for two adjustments.* First, the figure to be used as the n or N should always be the total number of *payments* in the problem, not the number of years. Second, the figure to be used as the interest rate should always be the *periodic* interest rate, not the annual rate. For example, in a problem that involves three years of quarterly payments and a 16 percent nominal annual interest rate compounded quarterly, n or N is 12, and the interest rate is 4 percent. Or, in one that involves five years of monthly

payments and a 6 percent nominal annual interest rate compounded monthly, n or N is 60, and the interest rate is .5 percent.

188.   A corporate bond is a frequently encountered security that includes a simple annuity with payments occurring other than annually.   For example, assume that a bond provides semiannual interest payments of $40 for ten years, beginning six months from now, as well as payment of the $1,000 principal sum at the end of the tenth year. If bonds with a similar degree of riskiness are yielding 11 percent, what should you pay for this bond? The present value of 20 payments of $40 each should be found based on a 5.5 percent discount rate. To this should be added the present value of the $1,000 final payment, also discounted at 5.5 percent for 20 periods. On a financial calculator, enter 40 as the end-of-period PMT, 1000 as the FV, 5.5 as the interest rate, 20 as the value of n or N, and find the PV, or intrinsic value of this bond, $820.74.[11]

189.   Now assume that you buy this bond for $821 and hold it for three years, at which time it is called by the issuing corporation for $1,040. What has been your annual yield to the call date? On a financial calculator, enter 821 as the PV, 1040 as the FV, 40 as the end-of-period PMT, and 6 as the value of n or N. Find the periodic interest rate, 8.47%. Find the nominal annual rate or APR or yield to call by doubling 8.47 to 16.94 percent. If you wish to be even more precise, you could convert this periodic rate to an *effective* annual rate. The effective annual yield to call of a nominal annual 16.94 percent received semiannually is 17.66 percent.

190.   You can also calculate the n or N, interest rate, or amount of the payment in a simple annuity or annuity due involving other-than-annual payments. Use the same tools as you would have used if the payments had been annual. Again, however, the item you input or compute as n or N will always be the total number of payments, not the total number of years. The item you input or compute as the interest rate will always be the periodic interest rate, not the annual rate. And, the item you input or compute as PMT will always be the single periodic payment, not the sum of the payments per year.

Complex Annuities and Complex Annuities Due

191.   A complex annuity or annuity due is one in which the frequency of payments and the frequency of compounding or discounting are different. For example, a series of 14 monthly deposits that are credited with interest daily and that begin immediately is a complex annuity due. Likewise, a series of ten semiannual lease payments that are discounted on an annual basis and that begin six months from now is a complex annuity.

192.   The mathematics of solving problems involving complex annuities are fairly complicated and generally beyond the scope of this book. Here, we will deal with only two types of complex annuity problems, computing the FVA or FVAD and the PVA or PVAD. The tool described for finding the solution to each will be a formula, though a calculator will also be needed, especially to facilitate raising certain numbers to a power.

193.   In order to solve problems involving complex annuities, it is necessary to introduce one new variable that has not been used in any of the problems heretofore. That new variable, which we shall label as "c," is the number of times that compounding or discounting occurs *in each payment interval*. The value of c is found by dividing the frequency of compounding or discounting per year by the frequency of the payments per year. For example, if compounding occurs monthly and annuity payments are made quarterly, $c = 3$. Or, if discounting occurs semiannually and annuity payments are made weekly, $c = 2/52 = 1/26$.

194.   The formula for computing the future value of a complex annuity is presented below. In it, as in simple annuities, i is the periodic interest rate, and n is the total number of annuity payments.

$$\text{FVA} = \left[\frac{(1+i)^{n \times c} - 1}{(1+i)^{c} - 1} \right] \quad \text{(Amount of one deposit)}$$

195.   To illustrate, assume that $70 is deposited in a savings account every six months for five years. The first deposit is made six months from now. Interest is credited to the account at a 12 percent nominal annual rate, compounded monthly. How much will be in the account at the end of five years? Substituting in the formula, we have:

$$\text{FVA} \quad = \quad \left[\frac{(1.01)^{10 \times 6} - 1}{(1.01)^6 - 1} \right] (\$70)$$

$$= \quad \left[\frac{.8167}{.0615} \right] (\$70)$$

$$= \quad 13.2797 \times \$70$$

$$= \quad \$929.58$$

196. If in this illustration the first deposit were made immediately, rather than six months from now, that is, if the problem called for finding FVAD, one further step would be necessary. The value of the FVA would have to be increased in a manner analogous to that used for annual annuities due. Specifically, the adjustment to be made is:

$$\text{FVAD} = \text{FVA} (1 + i)^c$$

Again, remember to use the periodic interest rate for i in making this adjustment. In this illustration, then:

$$\text{FVAD} \quad = \$929.58 (1.01)^6$$

$$= \$929.58 \times 1.0615$$

$$= \$986.75$$

That is, the account balance would be 6.15 percent higher because an extra six months of interest would be earned at a 12 percent nominal annual rate compounded monthly.

197. Next, we will turn to calculating the present value of a complex annuity. The formula is presented below. As before, n is the total number of payments, i is the periodic interest rate, and c is the discounting frequency per payment interval.

$$PVA = \left[\frac{1 - \frac{1}{(1+i)^{n \times c}}}{(1+i)^c - 1} \right] \quad \text{(Amount of one payment)}$$

198. To illustrate, assume that during the first three and one-half years after you retire, you want to have interest income of $250 per month, beginning one month after your retirement date. Also assume that the principal sum to be liquidated in order to provide this income can be invested at a nominal annual rate of 6 percent, compounded quarterly. How large a principal sum will you need on the date you retire? What is the present value of this complex annuity? Substituting in the formula, we have:

$$PVA = \left[\frac{1 - \frac{1}{(1.015)^{42 \times \frac{1}{3}}}}{(1.015)^{\frac{1}{3}} - 1} \right] \quad (\$250)$$

$$= \left[\frac{(1 - .8118)}{(1.0050 - 1)} \right] \quad (\$250)$$

$$= 37.64 \times \$250$$

$$= \$9,410.00$$

199. If in this illustration the $250 of monthly income were to begin on your retirement date, rather than one month later, that is, if the problem called for calculating the PVAD rather than the PVA, one further step would be necessary. The value of the PVA would have to be increased in a manner analogous to that used for annual annuities due. Specifically, the adjustment to be made is:

$$PVAD = PVA (1 + i)^c$$

Again, remember to use the periodic interest rate in making this adjustment. In this illustration, then:

$$PVAD = \$9,410 (1.015)^{\frac{1}{3}}$$

$$= \$9,410 (1.0050)$$

$$= \$9,457.05$$

That is, the principal sum would have to be about .5 percent higher because one month of interest earnings would be lost on a 6 percent annual rate compounded quarterly.

NOTES

1.   Most corporate bonds pay interest semiannually. For purposes of simplicity, however, annual payments will be assumed here. A later section of this chapter deals with compounding and discounting where cash flows occur more frequently than once per year.

2.   In some cases, you might at this point want to calculate an annuity, that is, a series of level payments, that would have the same net present value as the uneven cash flows in the machine. If so, simply press the NUS (net uniform series) menu key to produce the answer, $61,353.83. A five-year annuity of this amount, discounted as 12.5 percent, has a present value of $218,454.50.

3.   Alternatively, you could compute the present value under the end-of-year approach and multiply the result by $(1 + i)$.

4.   You may have noticed that this cash flow can be restated in terms that are easier to handle if you are using formulas.

> $30,000 for 10 years
> +$10,000 for 9 years
> +$10,000 for 8 years
> +$10,000 for 5 years

Compute the future value of each annuity and add them together.

5.   In this and in all investment opportunities being evaluated, care must be exercised to be sure that all relevant elements of the cash inflow and outflow streams are considered and discounted properly. Don't forget, for example, to include when appropriate such items as shipping and installation costs of a proposed new piece of equipment, maintenance costs, income taxes, salvage value, etc. In the illustrations in this portion of the chapter, it is assumed that all such considerations have already been accounted for in the numbers being used.

6.   As will be seen, this is not usually necessary when using the HP-12C, HP-10B II, HP-17B II, or BA-II Plus calculator's IRR function.

7.   For more on this phenomenon, review the subject of NPV profiles in college-level financial management textbooks.

8.   For an interesting example of multiple IRRs, see Roger H. Allen, *Real Estate Investment and Taxation*. 2nd ed. (Cincinnati: South-Western Publishing Co., 1984), p. 205. There, an illustration developed by Robert J. Doyle, formerly of the faculty of The American College, is presented, showing an investment that has several internal rates of return. The cash flows used in the illustration are ($1,000), $3,600, ($4,310), and $1,716. An investment with this set of cash flows has IRRs of 10 percent, 20 percent, and 30 percent. Each of those rates, when used to discount the cash flows, produces an NPV of zero.

9.   Financial institutions typically use a 360-day year as the basis for daily compounding calculations. This produces a slightly smaller annual interest, all other things being equal, than if they were to use a 365-day year.

10.   The mathematics of calculating the effective rate manually when compounding is continuous are too complex to be dealt with in this book. The procedure for calculating it by using the HP-12C, HP-10B II, HP-17B II, or BA-II Plus calculators, however, is included in Appendices A, B, C, and D.

11.   Except for the HP-10B II, the financial calculators dealt with in this text also have separate systems for computing various bond values. Consult the owner's manual for details.

PROBLEMS

1.   The divorce is final and you have been awarded the following alimony: $5,000 at the end of each of the next three years, plus $6,000 at the end of each of the following five years, plus $7,000 at the end of each of the following ten years. If you remarry, however, you receive no further alimony. Measured in terms of present value and a discount rate of 6.5 percent, what will your wedding cost if you remarry today?

2.   To convince yourself of the wisdom of your recent decision to quit smoking (and this time you really mean it), you plan at the end of each of the next five years to put into a savings account earning 6 percent compound annual interest the money you would have spent on cigarettes. You anticipate that the amounts of the five deposits will be $400, $450, $500, $550, and $600. If all goes according to plan, how much will be in your account after five years?

3.   Which of the following income streams would you rather have if interest rates currently are 7 percent?

Beginning of Year	Cash Flow		End of Year	Cash Flow
1	$2,000		1	0
2	$2,500		2	0
3	$3,000	OR	3	$5,500
4	$3,000		4	$5,500
5	$3,000		5	$5,500

4.   Your racehorse is a sure thing to win $60,000 for you at the end of each of the next three years, after which you believe that the horse will be able to earn about $10,000 per year in stud fees at the end of each of five years. If you insist on a compound annual rate of return of at least 20 percent, what would you accept for the horse today?

5.   Tuition at the university your daughter will be attending next year is expected to be $11,000 at that time and to rise by about 8 percent per year thereafter. You plan to set aside today a

capital sum that, invested at 6 percent interest, will be just sufficient to pay her tuition in full at the start of each of the four years. How large a capital sum will be needed to accomplish this objective?

6.   Your goal is to have accumulated a capital sum of $75,000 when you retire 12 years from now. You plan to make an initial deposit of $2,000 today, and on each of the following 11 annual anniversary dates, you will deposit an amount that is 10 percent higher than the previous year's deposit. If your deposits earn 7 percent interest per year, will you reach your goal?

7.   You have just made a loan of $85,000 to a friend, who has agreed to the following repayment schedule:

End of year 1	$ 5,000
End of year 2	$ 10,000
End of year 3	0
End of year 4	0
End of year 5	$100,000

(a)   What is your internal rate of return?

(b)   What is the net present value of this investment if 10 percent is your minimum acceptable compound annual rate of return?

8.   Tax reform legislation notwithstanding, you have located an exotic tax-sheltered investment opportunity. For an initial outlay of $50,000 and an additional $10,000 five years from now, you will receive the following income stream:

End of years 1-4	$7,500
End of years 6-10	$8,000

What is the internal rate of return on this investment?

9.   You are debating whether to invest $100,000 in a piece of equipment that will produce the following cost savings for your business:

End of years 1-3	$30,000
End of year 4	($10,000)
End of years 5-7	$20,000

    (a)   What is the internal rate of return?

    (b)   What is the net present value if you discount the cash flows at the 8 percent compound annual interest rate you would have to pay in order to finance the purchase of the equipment?

    (c)   What is the modified internal rate of return if a 5 percent reinvestment rate is assumed?

10.   Use the formula or your financial calculator to compute the effective annual interest rate when a nominal annual rate of 18 percent is compounded:

    (a)   Semiannually

    (b)   Quarterly

    (c)   Monthly

    Check your answers by comparing them with the table in Appendix E.

11.   Where should you put your money: in a certificate of deposit that will earn 9.75 percent compounded daily (360 days) or in one that will earn 10 percent compounded semiannually?

12.   (a)   Show which is the larger amount: the future value of a ten-year $2,000 annual annuity growing at a nominal annual interest rate of 5 percent compounded weekly or one growing at a nominal annual interest rate of 5 percent compounded monthly.

    (b)   Show which is the larger amount: the present value of a six-year $3,000 annual annuity discounted at 11 percent applied monthly or one discounted at 11 percent applied quarterly.

13.   Assume that you plan to save for Junior's college education by depositing $200 per month for the next 12 years in

a savings account, beginning immediately. The account is expected to earn a nominal annual rate of 6 percent, compounded monthly. How much will be in the account at the end of the twelfth year?

14.   What is the present value of a stream of ten quarterly payments of $500 each, beginning three months from now, if an annual discount rate of 16 percent is applied semiannually?

SOLUTIONS

1.   Not counting the cost of the gown, the organist, the flowers, the photographer, etc., the wedding will cost you $64,290.04. If you wish to use formulas, you should:

> (a)   Compute the PVA of the first series of payments.

> (b)   Compute the PVA of the second series of payments.

> (c)   Compute the PVSS of the PVA of the second series of payments.

> (d)   Compute the PVA of the third series of payments.

> (e)   Compute the PVSS of the PVA of the third series of payments.

> (f)   Add the results of (a), (c), and (e).

If you use a financial calculator, enter the first series of cash flows, which occur three times, starting at the end of the first year; then the next series of cash flows, which occur five times; then the third series of cash flows, which occur ten times; then the interest rate; then find NVP, which is $64,290.04.

2.   The future value of these five items of ungrouped data, based on the FVSS formula, will be as follows:

$$
\begin{array}{lcr}
\$400 \times 1.06^4 & = & \$\ 505.00 \\
\$450 \times 1.06^3 & = & 535.95 \\
\$500 \times 1.06^2 & = & 561.80 \\
\$550 \times 1.0600 & = & 583.00 \\
\$600 \times 1.0000 & = & \underline{600.00} \\
\end{array}
$$

Total future value $2,785.75

Use of a financial calculator in the way described in this chapter would produce a future value of the same amount. Find the PV and carry it forward as a single sum to an FV.

3.   If you use PVSS and PVA formulas, you should:

As regards the left-hand column:

(a)   Note the amount of the first cash flow.

(b)   Compute the PVSS of the second cash flow.

(c)   Compute the PVA of the next series of cash flows.

(d)   Compute the PVSS of that PVA.

(e)   Total the results of (a), (b), and (d), which will be about $11,694.

As regards the right-hand column:

(a)   Compute the PVA of the series of cash flows.

(b)   Compute the PVSS of this PVA, which will be about $12,606.

Or, if you use a financial calculator, enter the cash flows from the left-hand column in sequence, as well as the discount rate, and find the NPV, which is $11,694.34. Clear the machine and enter the cash flows for the right-hand column, beginning with zero until the end of the third year. Then enter the remaining cash flows and the discount rate. Solve for the NPV, which is $12,606.99.

4.   If you use PVSS and PVA formulas to compute the house's present value, you should:

(a)   Compute the PVA of the cash flows in the first three years.

(b)   Compute the PVA of the cash flows in the remaining five years.

(c)   Compute the PVSS of the PVA of the cash flows in the remaining five years.

(d)   Total the results of (a) and (c), which will be about $143,697, your minimum selling price.

Or, on a financial calculator, enter the cash flows in sequence, starting at the end of the first year. Then enter the discount rate and find the NPV, which is $143,695.67, your minimum selling price.

5.   The answer may be found through the formula for calculating the present value of a series of payments that grow by a constant percentage. Specifically:

$$\text{PV} \quad = (1.06) \left[\frac{1 - \left[\frac{1.08^4}{1.06} \right]}{(.06 - .08)} \right] \times \$11,000$$

$$= (1.06) \left[\frac{1 - 1.0776}{-.02} \right] \times \$11,000$$

$$= 1.06 \times 3.8817 \times \$11,000$$

$$= \$45,260.62$$

But, since the first payment is not due for one year, this result should be divided by 1.06 to produce the answer, $42,698.70.

Or, if you follow the sequence of keystrokes presented in paras. 53-56 of the chapter for the HP-12C, HP-10B II, HP-17B II, or BA-II Plus, the answer that appears on the display will be $45,261.02. Dividing this by 1.06 produces the answer, $42,699.08.

6.   You will not reach the $75,000 goal with the planned funding pattern. The answer may be found through the formula for calculating the future value of a series of deposits that grow by a constant percentage and that begin immediately. Specifically:

$$FV = (1.07) \left[\frac{(1.07)^{12} - (1.10)^{12}}{(.07) - (.10)} \right] \times \$2,000$$

$$= (1.07) \left[\frac{2.2522 - 3.1384}{-.03} \right] \times \$2,000$$

$$= 1.07 \times 29.5400 \times \$2,000$$

$$= \$63,215.60$$

Or, if you follow the sequence of keystrokes presented in paras. 69-73 of the chapter for the HP-12C, the HP-10B II, the HP-17B II, or the BA-II Plus, the answer that appears on the display will be $63,218.22.

7.   (a)   Even for a fairly simple set of cash flows such as this one, a financial calculator is the most practical means of calculating the IRR.

The keystrokes for the HP-12C are as follows: 85000, CHS, blue g, CFo, 5000, blue g, CFj, 10000, blue g, CFj, 0, blue g, CFj, 2, blue g, Nj, 100000, blue g, CFj, yellow f, IRR.

On the HP-10B II, press 85000, +/-, CF_j, 5000, CF_j, 10000, CF_j, 0, CF_j, 2, shift, N_j, 100000, CF_j, shift, IRR/YR.

On the HP-17B II, with the #T? function turned ON, the keystrokes in the CFLO menu system are as follows: 85000, +/-, INPUT, 5000, INPUT, 1, INPUT, 10000, INPUT, 1, INPUT, 0, INPUT, 2, INPUT, 100000, INPUT, 1, INPUT, EXIT, the CALC menu key, and the IRR% menu key.

The keystrokes for the BA-II Plus are as follows: 85000, +/-, ENTER, ↓, 5000, ENTER, ↓, ↓, 10000, ENTER, ↓, ↓, 0, ENTER, ↓, 2, ENTER, ↓, 100000, ENTER, ↓, IRR, CPT.

The answer is 6.9171%.

(b)   With the above data still in the machine, on the HP-12C press 10, i, yellow f, NPV.

On the HP-10B II, press 10, I/YR, shift, and NPV.

On the HP-17B II, press 10, the I% menu key, and the NPV menu key.

Or, on the BA-II Plus, press NPV, 10, ENTER, ↓, CPT.

The answer is -$10,097.95.

8.   On the HP-12C, press 50000, CHS, blue g, CFo, 7500, blue g, CFj, 4, blue g, Nj, 10000, CHS, blue g, CFj, 8000, blue g, CFj, 5, blue g, Nj, yellow f, IRR.

On the HP-10B II, press 50000, +/-, CF_j, 7500, CF_j, 4, shift, N_j, 10000, +/-, CF_j, 8000, CF_j, 5, shift, N_j, shift, IRR/YR.

On the HP-17B II, the keystrokes in the CFLO menu system with the #T? function turned on are as follows: 50000, +/-, INPUT, 7500, INPUT, 4, INPUT, 10000, +/-, INPUT, 1, INPUT, 8000, INPUT, 5, INPUT, EXIT, the CALC menu key, and the IRR% menu key.

On the BA-II Plus, press 50000, +/-, ENTER, ↓, 7500, ENTER, ↓, 4, ENTER, ↓, 10000, +/-, ENTER, ↓, ↓, 8000, ENTER, ↓, 5, ENTER, ↓, IRR, CPT.

The answer probably is 3.3231%. Because the income stream involves more than one sign change, however, there may be more than one IRR, though this is unlikely.

9.   (a)   The internal rate of return may be found on the HP-12C by pressing 100000, CHS, blue g, CFo, 30000, blue g, CFj, 3, blue g, Nj, 10000, CHS, blue g, CFj, 20000, blue g, CFj, 3, blue g, Nj, yellow f, IRR.

If you are using the HP-10B II, press 100000, +/-, CF_j, 30000, CF_j, 3, shift, N_j, 10000, +/-, CF_j, 20000, CF_j, 3, shift, N_j, shift, IRR/YR.

If you are using the HP-17B II, you can find the IRR by entering the CFLO menu system, turning on the #T? function, and pressing the following keys: 100000, +/-, INPUT,

30000, INPUT, 3, INPUT, 10000, +/-, INPUT, 1, INPUT, 20000, INPUT, 3, INPUT, EXIT, the CALC menu key, and the IRR% menu key.

Or, you can find the IRR on the BA-II Plus by pressing 100000, +/-, ENTER, ↓, 30000, ENTER, ↓, 3, ENTER, ↓, 10000, +/-, ENTER, ↓, ↓, 20000, ENTER, ↓, 3, ENTER, ↓, IRR, CPT.

The answer is 10.6118% (but see solution 8 above, this chapter).

(b)   With the above data still in the HP-12C, press 8, i, yellow f, NPV.

On the HP-10B II, press 8, I/YR, shift, NPV.

On the HP-17B, press 8, the I% menu key, and the NPV menu key.

Or, if you use the BA-II Plus, with the above data still in the machine, press NPV, 8, ENTER, ↓, CPT.

The answer is $7,847.48.

(c)   The future or terminal value of the inflows at 5 percent is $30,000 for 6 years, 5 years, and 4 years, plus $20,000 for two years and 1 year, plus $20,000. These total $178,006.51. The present value of the outflows is $100,000, plus $10,000 discounted at 5 percent for 4 years. These total $108,227.02. The MIRR between these two values in 7 years is 7.3672%.

10.   (a) $\left[1 + \dfrac{.18}{2}\right]^2 - 1 = 18.8100\%$

     (b) $\left[1 + \dfrac{.18}{4}\right]^4 - 1 = 19.2519\%$

     (c) $\left[1 + \dfrac{.18}{12}\right]^{12} - 1 = 19.5618\%$

11.   Take the 10 percent rate. The 9.75 percent CD pays an effective rate of:

$$\left[1 + \dfrac{.0975}{360}\right]^{360} - 1 = 10.2397\%$$

Whereas, the 10 percent CD pays an effective rate of:

$$\left[1 + \dfrac{.10}{2}\right]^2 - 1 = 10.2500\%$$

12.   (a)   Weekly compounding will produce the larger FVA because the effective annual interest rate is 5.1246 percent, versus 5.1162 percent for monthly compounding. Substituting these effective rates in the FVA formula, we have:

$$\left[\dfrac{1.051246^{10} - 1}{.051246}\right] (\$2,000) = \$25,302.57$$

Versus

$$\left[\dfrac{1.051162^{10} - 1}{.051162}\right] (\$2,000) = \$25,292.64$$

(b)   Discounting on a quarterly basis will produce the larger PVA. The effective rate for quarterly discounting is 11.4621 percent, versus 11.5719 percent for monthly discounting. Substituting these effective rates in the PVA formula, we have:

$$\left[\frac{1 - \dfrac{1}{(1.114621)^6}}{.114621} \right] (\$3,000) = \$12,524.44$$

versus

$$\left[\frac{1 - \dfrac{1}{(1.115719)^6}}{.115719} \right] (\$3,000) = \$12,485.23$$

13.   If you use the **FVAD** formula, the answer for this simple annuity is found as:

$$= (1.005) \left[\frac{(1.005)^{144} - 1}{.005} \right] (\$200)$$

$$= (1.005) \left[\frac{1.0508}{.005} \right] (\$200)$$

$$= 1.005 \times 210.16 \times \$200$$

$$= \$42,242.16$$

The HP-12C, HP-10B II, HP-17B II, or BA-II Plus can also be used. Remember that n or N is 144, and the interest rate is .5. The answer displayed will be $42,240.18.

14.   In this problem the annuity is a complex annuity. The value of c is $2 \div 4$, or 1/2. Substituting in the formula for the PVA of a complex annuity, we have:

$$= \left[\frac{1 - \dfrac{1}{(1.08)^{10 \times 1/2}}}{(1.08)^{1/2} - 1} \right] (\$500)$$

$$= \left[\frac{1 - .6806}{.0392} \right] (\$500)$$

$$= 8.1480 \times \$500$$

$$= \$4,074.00$$

Chapter Three

Time Value of Money: Self-Test

Presented below are a number of multiple choice questions through which you can test your understanding of the material in the preceding two chapters. For each of these questions, circle what you think is the correct answer. When you have completed the self-test, check your answers against those in the answer key that follows the questions. For any on which you gave an incorrect answer, see the explanation that follows the answer key. Also, you may wish to review the section of the chapter that explains the correct answer by using the text reference that accompanies each question.

QUESTIONS

1.   According to the concept of the time value of money, which of the following statements are correct?

(Ch. 1, para. 1-5)

(1)   When paying your federal income taxes, it is better to pay early rather than at the last moment.

(2)   When collecting your monthly salary, it is better to collect it as early as possible rather than later.

(3)   A customer who pays you at the last possible moment is one who recognizes the opportunity cost of money.

(4)   People prefer to pay later rather than sooner to gain the use of the money during the delay.

A.   (1), (2), and (3) only
B.   (2), (3), and (4) only
C.   (1) and (2) only
D.   (3) and (4) only
E.   (1), (2), (3), and (4)

2.   Thrifty Thelma has $5,000 to invest. One investment opportunity offers her 10% simple interest for five years. The second investment opportunity offers her 10% compound interest for five years. At the end of the five years, the simple interest will cause her $5,000 to grow to ___, and the compound interest will cause her $5,000 to grow to ___, respectively.

(Ch. 1, para. 11-14)

A. $5,250 and $7,500
B. $6,000 and $7,000
C. $7,500 and $8,052.55
D. $7,500 and $8,144.47
E. $7,687.45 and $9,112.68

3.   Which of the following statements concerning compounding or discounting is correct?

(Ch. 1, para. 16-19)

A.   Discounting is the process by which a present value grows to a larger future value.
B.   As the number of periods or the interest rate in a time-value-of-money problem is increased, the present value of a future sum is reduced.
C.   The term "discounting" is essentially a synonym for the term "compounding."
D.   In the compounding process, the future value grows by an increasing percentage each period.
E.   As the number of periods or the interest rate in a time-value-of-money problem is increased, the future value of a present sum is reduced.

4.   Which of the following statements concerning the frequency of compounding or discounting is (are) correct?

(Ch. 1, para. 25-27)

(1)   If compounding occurs semiannually, the future value of a sum of money will be lower than if compounding occurs annually.

(2)   If discounting occurs semiannually, the present value of a sum of money will be lower than if discounting occurs annually.

(3)   The greater the frequency of compounding or discounting per year, the greater will be the effect on a future or present value.

A.   (1), (2), and (3)   D.   (1) only
B.   (2) and (3) only   E.   (2) only
C.   (1) and (3) only

5.   If the future value of a single sum (FVSS) is found by multiplying the present value by $(1.12)^{11}$, then the interest rate and duration, respectively, are:

(Ch. 1, para. 40)

A.   11% and 11 periods
B.   11% and 12 periods
C.   12% and 11 periods
D.   12% and 12 periods
E.   None of the above

6.   Which of the following statements concerning the future value of a single sum (FVSS) is (are) correct?

(Ch. 1, para. 43-44)

(1)   The higher the interest rate, the lower the FVSS.
(2)   The longer the duration, the lower the FVSS.
(3)   Multiplying a present value by $(1+i)^n$ produces the future value of a single sum.

A.   (1), (2), and (3)   D.   (1) only
B.   (1) and (2) only   E.   (3) only
C.   (2) and (3) only

7.   Lois has some money to invest. One investment opportunity offers her 4% compound interest for the next four years, and the second investment opportunity offers her 8% compound interest for the same four years. Which of the following statements is correct?

(Ch. 1, para. 43-44)

A.   Since 8% is exactly double 4%, the amount of interest earned over the four years will be exactly double at 8%.

B.   Because of compounding, interest at the 4% rate will be more than half the interest at the 8% rate.

C.   Because of compounding, interest at the 8% rate will be more than double the interest at the 4% rate.

D.   Because of compounding, interest at the 8% rate will be less than double the interest at the 4% rate.

E.   It is impossible to compare the interest that will be earned without knowing the amount of money Lois has to invest.

8.   Richard has some money to invest. One investment opportunity offers him 6% compound interest over the next six years. The second investment opportunity offers him 6% compound interest over the next 12 years. Which of the following statements is correct?

(Ch. 1, para. 43-44)

A.   Since 12 years is exactly double six years, the amount of interest over the 12 years will be exactly double that for six years.

B.   Because of compounding, the amount of interest for 12 years will be more than double that for six years.

C.   Because of compounding, the amount of interest for 12 years will be less than double that for six years.

D.   Because of compounding, the total amount of interest earned on either opportunity will be the same.

E.   It is impossible to compare the interest that will be earned without knowing the amount of money that Richard has to invest.

9.   Which the following must be known to compute the future value of a single sum?

(Ch. 1, para. 40)

(1)   The mean value
(2)   The present value
(3)   The number of time periods
(4)   The interest rate
(5)   The periodic payment

A.   (2), (3), (4), and (5) only
B.   (1), (3), (4), and (5) only
C.   (3), (4), and (5) only
D.   (2), (3), and (4) only
E.   (1) only

10.   Which of the following formulas describes the relationship between the present and future value of a single sum of money?

(Ch. 1, para. 40)

A. $PVSS + FVSS = (1 + n)^i$
B. $PVSS = FVSS (1 + n)^i$
C. $PVSS = FVSS (1 + i)^n$
D. $FVSS = PVSS (1 + i)^n$
E. $PVSS + FVSS = (1 + i)^n$

11.   Frances can invest $6,000 at compound annual interest of 7%. Approximately how long will she have to wait to have $12,000?

(Ch. 1, para. 78-81)

A.   Between seven and eight years
B.   Between eight and nine years
C.   Between nine and ten years
D.   Between ten and eleven years
E.   Between eleven and twelve years

12.   Jane can invest $4,000 for nine years. Approximately what rate of compound interest will she have to earn to double her money to $8,000?

(Ch. 1, para. 78-95)

A.   About 7%
B.   About 8%
C.   About 9%
D.   About 10%
E.   About 11%

13.   Jonathan has just been told that he has inherited some money from the estate of his late grandmother. Under the terms of the will, Jonathan has to choose one of three options:

(1) $50,000 today and $60,000 five years from today

(2) $50,000 today and $70,000 ten years from today

(3) $50,000 today and $80,000 fifteen years from today

If Jonathan's opportunity cost of money is 6%, which of the following statements is correct advice for Jonathan?

(Ch. 1, para. 96-114)

A.   Option (1) is the best choice.
B.   Option (3) is the best choice.
C.   Option (2) is the best choice.
D.   Option (1) is the worst choice.
E.   Option (2) is the worst choice.

14.   If the present value of a single sum (PVSS) of $1.00 is $.50187, which can be represented by:

$$\frac{1}{(1.09)^8}$$

Then the interest rate and duration, respectively, are:

(Ch. 1, para. 98)

A.   9% and 8 periods
B.   9% and 9 periods
C.   8% and 8 periods
D.   8% and 9 periods
E.   1.99% and 1 year

15.   Which of the following statements concerning the present value of a single sum (PVSS) is (are) correct?

(Ch. 1, para.101)

(1)   The higher the interest rate, the higher the PVSS.
(2)   The longer the duration, the higher the PVSS.
(3)   Durations and interest rates have no effect on PVSS.

A.   (1), (2), and (3)
B.   (1) only
C.   (2) only
D.   (3) only
E.   Neither (1), (2), nor (3)

16.   The present value of a single sum (PVSS) can be calculated by using which of the following formulas?

(Ch. 1, para. 98)

A. $PVSS = \dfrac{FVSS}{(1+i)^n}$

B. $PVSS = \dfrac{(1+i)^n}{FVSS}$

C. $PVSS = (1+i)^n \times FVSS$

D. $PVSS = \left[\dfrac{FVSS}{(1+n)^i \times FVSS} \right]$

E. $PVSS = (1+n)^i \times FVSS$

17.   Roger borrowed money from Lionel a few years ago, and Roger is scheduled to repay the money, with interest, seven years from today, an amount that will then be $12,000. However, Lionel has just heard from his accountant that he (Lionel) must pay a tax assessment of $5,500 tomorrow. Accordingly, Lionel offers Roger the opportunity to pay $5,500 today rather than $12,000 seven years from today. What annual rate of interest is Lionel using in discounting Roger's obligation?

(Ch. 1, para. 116-120)

A.   Between 11% and 12%
B.   Between 12% and 13%
C.   Between 13% and 14%
D.   Between 14% and 15%
E.   Approximately 21%

18.   Ted has borrowed $12,000 by agreeing to repay $30,000 at a specified date in the future, using an interest rate of 11%. For how many years has Ted borrowed this money?

(Ch. 1, para. 121-124)

A.   Just over eight years
B.   Just under nine years
C.   Just over nine years
D.   Just under ten years
E.   Just over ten years

19.   Which of the following statements concerning an annuity is correct?

(Ch. 1, para. 126)

A.   An annuity is a series of increasing payments or receipts at the end of each of a specified number of periods.

B.   An annuity is a series of increasing payments or receipts at the beginning of each of a specified number of periods.

C.   An annuity is a series of level payments or receipts at the end of each of a specified number of periods.

D.   An annuity is a series of level payments or receipts at the beginning of each of a specified number of periods.

E.   An annuity is a series of payments or receipts that grow by a constant percentage.

20.   Which of the following statements concerning annuities is correct?

(Ch. 1, para. 126-127)

A.   An annuity is a mathematical concept involving periodic payments and interest.

B.   An annuity due involves periodic payments, interest, and mortality.

C.   An annuity involves periodic payments that are made at the beginning of each period.

D.   An annuity may involve periodic payments, but not periodic receipts.

E.   An annuity lasts for the lifetime of an individual.

21.   Which of the following are examples of annuities?

(Ch. 1, para. 127)

(1)   Equal monthly deposits into a savings account
(2)   Mortgage payments by a homeowner to a bank
(3)   The monthly earnings of a typical life insurance agent or stockbroker
(4)   Automobile payments by a car owner to a finance company

A.	(1), (2), (3), and (4)	D.	(1) and (2) only
B.	(2), (3), and (4) only	E.	(3) and (4) only
C.	(1), (2), and (4) only		

22.   Wendy plans to deposit $1,000 into a savings account at the end of each of the next five years. The deposits will earn 7% compound annual interest. If Wendy follows through with her plan, approximately how much will be in her account immediately after the fifth deposit is made?

(Ch. 1, para. 132-151)

A. $5,403
B. $5,751
C. $6,153
D. $6,311
E. $6,602

23.   If, in the preceding question, Wendy were to make her five annual deposits beginning immediately, how would her account balance at the end of the fifth year be affected?

(Ch. 1, para. 132-151)

A.   It would be $1,500 higher.
B.   It would be 5% higher.
C.   It would be 7% higher.
D.   It would be $1,903 higher.
E.   It would be 20% higher.

24.   If you want to calculate the future value of level deposits of $1,250 per year, you would need to know which of the following?

(Ch. 1, para. 128-131)

(1)   The number of deposits to be made
(2)   The interest rate the deposits will earn
(3)   The timing of the first deposit

A.   (2) only   C.   (1) and (3) only
B.   (1) and (2) only   D.   (1), (2), and (3)

25.   The future value of an annuity of $1,000 annually for 15 years at 10% interest is $31,772.48. If this was, instead, an annuity due, its future value would be which of the following?

(Ch. 1, para. 128-131)

A. $28,884.07
B. $34,949.73
C. $32,772.48
D. $32,872.48
E. $28,595.23

26.   Hopeful Harry wants to be a millionaire 20 years from now when he will be aged 65. Assume that Harry can earn 8% on any periodic deposits. How much will Harry have to deposit at the end of each year to reach his $1,000,000 goal?

(Ch. 1, para. 155-161)

A. $80,000.00
B. $50,000.00
C. $21,852.21
D. $46,000.00
E.   Cannot be calculated with the information provided.

27.   Which of the following statements concerning the type of problem illustrated in Question 26 above is correct?

(Ch. 1, para. 155-161)

A.   It is an annuity due type of problem.

B.   It is a sinking fund type of problem.

C.   The required payments would be lower if the interest rate were 6%.

D.   The FVA cannot be computed on a financial calculator.

E.   The required payments would be lower if the number of years were 15.

28.   If Mark is trying to calculate the present value of a series of level $1,000 payments for 14 years at 10% interest, the PVA would be which of the following?

(Ch. 1, para. 183-194)

A. $7,366.69
B. $8,103.36
C. $8,418.09
D. $8,673.02
E. $9,001.93

29.   If instead of an ordinary annuity, Mark had been interested in calculating the present value of an annuity due in Question 28 above, the result would be:

(Ch. 1, para. 183-194)

A. $7,366.69
B. $8,103.36
C. $8,418.09
D. $8,673.02
E. $9,001.93

30.   Which of the following statements concerning the present value of an annuity or annuity due is correct?

(Ch. 1, para. 175-179)

A.   An increase in the interest rate used will increase the present value.

B.   If payments are to be made at the end of each year, it is an annuity due.

C.   If payments are to be made at the beginning of each year, it is an annuity.

D.   The present value of an annuity is greater than the present value of an annuity due.

E.   If annual deposits of $1,000 are made beginning immediately, it is an annuity due.

31.   Rocky has borrowed money from a bank for the purchase of a motorcycle. Under the terms of the loan, Rocky is to repay the bank by a series of equal annual sums at the end of each of the next four years. Rocky's payments may be classified as which of the following?

(Ch. 1, para. 173-174)

A.   An annuity
B.   A deferred annuity
C.   An annuity due
D.   A life annuity
E.   None of the above

32.   John borrowed $10,000 from a bank to be used to replace the roof on some investment property. The loan is at 8% interest for ten years. The amount of each equal annual payment that John will have to make is which of the following?

(Ch. 1, para. 203-207)

A. $1,507.11
B. $1,490.29
C. $1,379.90
D. $1,080.00
E.   Impossible to calculate from information given.

33. Which of the following statements concerning an amortization schedule is (are) correct?

(Ch. 1, para. 221-224)

(1) It shows a declining beginning balance.
(2) It shows a declining ending balance.
(3) The annual interest amount rises each year.

A. (1), (2), and (3)   D. (2) only
B. (1) and (2) only   E. (3) only
C. (2) and (3) only

34. Diane is considering an investment that is expected to produce the following cash inflows:

End of Year	Amount
1	$1,000
2	1,000
3	3,000
4	4,000
5	4,000

If her opportunity cost of money is 8%, what is the most that Diane should be willing to pay for this investment?

(Ch. 2, para. 2-32)

A. $6,578.91
B. $8,279.42
C. $9,827.21
D. $13,000.00
E. $13,111.14

35. The last two cash flows in Question 34 above may be classified as:

(Ch. 2, para. 6)

A. Annuity due cash flows
B. Internal rate of return cash flows
C. Ungrouped cash flows
D. Grouped cash flows
E. None of the above

36.   Under the terms of a liability lawsuit settlement, Agnes is to be paid $10,000 today and then $6,000 at the end of each of the next nine years. If Agnes' opportunity cost of money is 7%, how much is the present value of her settlement?

(Ch. 2, para. 4-32)

A.   Approximately $29,000
B.   Approximately $39,000
C.   Approximately $49,000
D.   Approximately $59,000
E.   Approximately $69,000

37.   Karen wants to set aside today a capital sum to be liquidated over the next ten years for the care of her aged mother. The desired income stream for her mother is $20,000 beginning after one year and rising by 5% per year each year thereafter. Karen believes the investment earnings on the fund will be 8% per year. Approximately how large a capital sum must be set aside today to provide the desired income for Karen's mother?

(Ch. 2, para. 50-56)

A. $163,000
B. $172,000
C. $189,000
D. $202,000
E. $209,000

38.   Larry plans to begin saving for his children's education by depositing $2,000 today in a savings account. He plans to increase his annual deposits by 10% each year, beginning one year from now. He will make a total of six deposits, including the initial $2,000. If his account earns 6% interest per year, approximately how much will be in the account at the end of six years?

(Ch. 2, para. 66-73)

A. $15,700
B. $16,700
C. $17,700
D. $18,700
E. $19,700

39.   The net present value of an investment opportunity is calculated by:

(Ch. 2, para. 79-80)

A.   Subtracting all money outflows from all money inflows

B.   Subtracting the present value of money outflows from the present value of money inflows

C.   Adding the present value of money outflows to the present value of money inflows

D.   Subtracting all money outflows from all money inflows and multiplying the result by the PVA factor for the number of years and interest rate that are applicable

E.   Multiplying the initial outflow by the investment opportunity's IRR

40.   Jason's opportunity cost of money is 9%. He is contemplating an investment project with the following pattern of money flows:

Beginning of Year	Money Flow
1	$20,000 outflow
2	5,000 outflow
3	1,000 inflow
4	12,000 inflow
5	30,000 inflow

What is the approximate net present value of this investment opportunity to Jason?

(Ch. 2, para. 84-101)

A. $6,773
B. $24,587
C. $31,360
D. $55,947
E. $58,004

41. Which of the following statements concerning the internal rate of return is (are) correct?

(Ch. 2, para. 109)

(1) It is the discount rate that makes the present value of the money inflows exactly equal to the present value of the money outflows.

(2) It is the discount rate that makes the net present value exactly equal to zero.

(3) If it exceeds the investor's required rate of return, the investment is an attractive one.

A. (1), (2), and (3)   D. (2) and (3) only
B. (1) and (2) only   E. (3) only
C. (1) and (3) only

42. Which of the following statements concerning the similarity of the net present value and the internal rate of return techniques is (are) correct?

(Ch. 2, para. 82-83)

(1) As a rule, they both lead an investor to an identical conclusion when identical data are used.

(2) Should the two techniques indicate different conclusions, the net present value result is normally less reliable than the internal rate of return result.

(3) In both, the calculation requires that the investor specify the discount rate to be used.

A. (1), (2), and (3)   D. (2) and (3) only
B. (1) and (3) only   E. (1) only
C. (2) and (3) only

43.   In evaluating a proposed investment project, an investor should include in the analysis which of the following considerations?

(Ch. 2, para. 76)

(1)   The riskiness of the cash flows
(2)   The opportunity cost of money
(3)   The federal income tax treatment of the potential earnings

A.   (1), (2), and (3)   D.   (2) and (3) only
B.   (1) and (2) only   E.   (2) only
C.   (1) and (3) only

44.   Eric is considering two potential investment projects, each involving a lump-sum outlay now of $25,000 and no further outlays later. The first project is very risky and is expected to produce a net present value, based on a 5% discount rate, of $4,000. The second project is very safe and is expected to produce a net present value, based on a 5% discount rate, of –$4,000. In this situation, which of the following statements is definitely correct?

(Ch. 2, para. 79-81)

A.   The first project should be accepted.
B.   The second project should be rejected.
C.   Both projects should be accepted.
D.   Neither project should be accepted.
E.   The first project should be rejected.

45.   A proposed investment project has the following expected cash flows:

Initial outlay	–$20,000
End of Year 1	$5,000
End of Year 2	–$3,000
End of Year 3	$35,000

If a reinvestment rate of 7% is used, what is this project's approximate modified internal rate of return (MIRR)?

(Ch. 2, para. 136-139)

A.   7%
B.   17%
C.   22%
D.   25%

46.   The compounding of interest more frequently than annually results in which of the following?

(Ch. 2, para. 143-145)

A.   The introduction of interest into conversion
B.   The rapid conversion of interest into principal
C.   The rapid conversion of principal into interest
D.   The usefulness of the rule of 72
E.   None of the above

47. Which of the following statements concerning the compounding of interest is (are) correct?

(Ch. 2, para. 145)

(1) The greater the frequency of compounding, the smaller the amount of interest earned when each compounding occurs.

(2) As a borrower, all else being equal, you would prefer a loan with monthly compounding rather than the same loan with quarterly compounding.

(3) As a saver, all else being equal, you would prefer an account with daily compounding to one with monthly compounding.

A. (1), (2), and (3)   D. (2) and (3) only
B. (1) and (2) only   E. (3) only
C. (1) and (3) only

48. The nominal annual interest rate and the effective annual rate are identical when compounding occurs:

(Ch. 2, para. 148)

A. Quarterly
B. Continuously
C. Annually
D. Daily
E. Monthly

49. If a nominal 6% interest rate is compounded monthly, the effective annual interest rate is:

(Ch. 2, para. 150-155)

A. 5.9%
B. 6.00%
C. 6.17%
D. 6.34%
E. 6.82%

50.   Which of the following statements concerning the effect of compounding or discounting frequency on future or present values is (are) correct?

(Ch. 2, para. 160-162)

(1)   The more frequently compounding occurs, the greater will be the future value of a single sum or of an annuity.

(2)   The more frequently discounting occurs, the greater will be the present value of a single sum.

(3)   The more frequently discounting occurs, the greater will be the present value of an annuity.

A.   (1), (2), and (3)   (D)   (1) only
B.   (1) and (3) only   (E)   (2) only
C.   (2) and (3) only

51.   To calculate the future value of a single sum, with interest compounded quarterly, you should use which of the following formulas?

(Ch. 2, para. 169-170)

A. $FVSS = PVSS \times \left[\dfrac{(1+i)}{q} \right]^{qn}$

B. $FVSS = PVSS \times \left[\dfrac{(1+i)}{2} \right]^{2n}$

C. $FVSS = PVSS \times \left[\dfrac{(1-i)}{4} \right]^{4n}$

D. $FVSS = PVSS \times \left[1 + \dfrac{i}{4} \right]^{4n}$

E. $FVSS = \dfrac{PVSS \times 4}{(1+i)^{n}}$

52.   If a problem assumes an annual interest rate of 12% compounded quarterly for eight years, which of the following combinations should you use?

(Ch. 2, para. 168-170)

A.   16 periods at 1%
B.   32 periods at 12%
C.   32 periods at 3%
D.   16 periods at 6%
E.   None of the above

53.   Which of the following is an example of a simple annuity due?

(Ch. 2, para. 186)

A.   A series of five uneven monthly cash flows, beginning immediately, on which interest is compounded daily

B.   A series of five level monthly cash flows, beginning immediately, on which interest is compounded monthly

C.   A series of five level monthly cash flows, beginning after one month, on which interest is compounded monthly

D.   A series of five level monthly cash flows, beginning immediately, on which interest is compounded once per year

E.   None of the above

ANSWER KEY

1.	B	26.	C
2.	C	27.	B
3.	B	28.	A
4.	B	29.	B
5.	C	30.	E
6.	E	31.	A
7.	C	32.	B
8.	B	33.	B
9.	D	34.	C
10.	D	35.	D
11.	D	36.	C
12.	B	37.	A
13.	A	38.	D
14.	A	39.	B
15.	E	40.	A
16.	A	41.	A
17.	A	42.	E
18.	B	43.	A
19.	C	44.	B
20.	A	45.	C
21.	C	46.	B
22.	B	47.	C
23.	C	48.	C
24.	D	49.	C
25.	B	50.	D
		51.	D
		52.	C
		53.	B

EXPLANATIONS

1. B is the answer. It is to your advantage to pay at the last moment because of the time value of money in your possession, so (1) is incorrect.

2. C is the answer. Simple interest would add $500 a year, or a total of $2,500, to the original $5,000. Compound interest would add an increasing amount each year, totaling $3,052.55, to the original $5,000. Enter $5,000 as the PV, 10 as the i, and 5 as the n, and solve for FV = $8,052.55.

3. B is the answer. Discounting is the reverse of compounding and refers to the process of reducing a known future value to its present value. Therefore, A and C are incorrect. In compounding, the future value grows by an increasing amount, not percentage, so D is incorrect. E is incorrect because the future value rises as the number of periods or the interest rate rises.

4. B is the answer. (1) is incorrect because semiannual compounding produces a larger future value than annual compounding, all other things being equal.

5. C is the answer. The figure after the decimal point is the interest rate, and the exponent outside the parentheses is the number of periods.

6. E is the answer. (1) is incorrect because the higher is the interest rate, the larger is FVSS. (2) is incorrect because the higher is the number of periods, the larger is FVSS.

7. C is the answer. For example, the FVSS of $1.00 at 8% and four years is $1.3605. For 4% and four years, it is $1.1699. Note that $.3605 is more than double $.1699. Therefore, A, B, D, and E are incorrect.

8. B is the answer. Compounding results in an increasing amount of interest credited each year, so the interest earned in the final six years will be significantly greater than that earned in the first six years. Therefore, A, C, D, and E are incorrect.

9.   D is the answer. The known variables in an FVSS problem are PVSS, n or N, and the interest rate. (1) is a nonsense option, and (5) is needed only in annuity and uneven-cash flow problems.

10.   D is the answer because it shows the correct formula for computing FVSS based on a known PVSS.

11.   D is the answer. According to the rule of 72, the money will double in approximately 10.3 years (72 divided by 7 = 10.29).

12.   B is the answer. According to the rule of 72, 8% is needed because 72 ÷ 8 = 9 years. Or, on a calculator, enter 4000 as PV, 8000 as FV, and 9 as n or N. The interest rate is 8.01%.

13.   A is the answer. Based on a 6% discount rate, the PVSS of $60,000 in five years is $44,835.49. The PVSS of $70,000 in ten years is $39,087.63. The PVSS of $80,000 in 15 years is $33,381.20. Therefore, option (1) is the best choice, and option (3) is the worst choice.

14.   A is the answer. The number after the decimal point is the interest rate. The exponent outside the parentheses is the number of periods.

15.   E is the answer. (1) and (2) are incorrect because as the interest rate and the number of periods rise, PVSS falls. Therefore, (3) is also incorrect.

16.   A is the answer because it shows the correct formula for calculating PVSS based on a known FVSS. Compare this formula with that in option (D) of Question 10 above. Each of the two formulas is the reciprocal of the other.

17.   A is the answer. On a calculator, enter 12000 as FV, 5500 as PV, and 7 as n or N. The interest rate is 11.8%.

18.   B is the answer. On a calculator, enter 12000 as PV, 30000 as FV, and 11 as the interest rate. The value of n is rounded up to 9 on the HP-12C, and is 8.7801 on the HP-10B II, HP-17B II, or BA-II Plus.

19.   C is the answer. A is incorrect because an annuity is a series of level payments. B is incorrect for the same reason and because annuity payments occur at the end of each period. D is incorrect because annuity payments occur at the end of each period. E describes a serial payment, not an annuity. Serial payments are described in Chapter 2.

20.   A is the answer. An annuity due involves periodic payments or receipts at the beginning of each period. Mortality rates are not normally relevant. Therefore, B, C, and D are incorrect. E is incorrect because a life annuity lasts for a lifetime.

21.   C is the answer. An agent's or broker's monthly earnings typically are not level, so they do not constitute an annuity. Therefore, (3) is incorrect.

22.   B is the answer. On a calculator, enter 1000 as the end-of-period PMT, 7 as the interest rate, and 5 as n or N. FVA = $5,750.74.

23.   C is the answer. An FVAD is higher than an FVA by one year's interest earnings, all other things being equal.

24.   D is the answer. All three variables must be known to compute FVA or FVAD.

25.   B is the answer. $31,722.48 x 1.10 = $34,949.73.

26.   C is the answer. The sinking fund payment is found on a calculator by entering 1000000 as FV, 8 as the interest rate, and 20 as n or N. The end-of-period payment is $21,852.21.

27.   B is the answer. A is incorrect because the payments will be made at the end of the period, not the beginning as in an annuity due. C and E are incorrect because these would increase the required payments. D is also incorrect, as was demonstrated in the answer to 26.

28.   A is the answer. With $1,000 as the end-of-period PMT, 10% as the interest rate, and 14 as the n or N, PVA = $7,366.69.

29.   B is the answer. Change the setting to beginning-of-period PMTs. PVAD = $8,103.36.

30.   E is the answer. A is incorrect because it will reduce PV. B is incorrect because it is an annuity. C is incorrect because it is an annuity due. D is incorrect because PVAD is greater than PVA, as shown in the answer to the preceding two questions.

31.   A is the answer. B is incorrect because a deferred annuity is one that begins more than one payment period into the future. C is incorrect because Rocky's payments are to be made at the end of each period. D is incorrect because the loan payments must be continued even if Rocky dies before the four years are over.

32.   B is the answer. On a financial calculator, enter 10000 as PV, 8 as the interest rate, and 10 as n or N. The end-of-period PMT is $1,490.29.

33.   B is the answer. (3) is incorrect because as the loan is amortized, the amount of interest charged each year declines.

34.   C is the answer.

        On the HP-12C, press 1000, blue g, CFj, 2, blue g, Nj, 3000, blue g, CFj, 4000, blue g, CFj, 2, blue g, Nj, 8, i, yellow f, NPV.

        On the HP-10B II, press 0, CF_j, 1000, CF_j, 2, shift, N_j, 3000, CF_j, 4000, CF_j, 2, shift, N_j, 8, I/YR, shift, NPV.

        On the HP-17B II, press the following keys with the #T? function on: CFLO menu key, shift, CLEAR DATA, YES menu key, 0, INPUT, 1000, INPUT, 2, INPUT, 3000, INPUT, 1, INPUT, 4000, INPUT, 2, INPUT, EXIT, CALC menu key, 8, I% menu key, NPV menu key.

        On the BA-II Plus, press CF, Enter, ↓, 1000, Enter, ↓, 2, Enter, ↓, 3000, Enter, ↓, ↓, 4000, Enter, ↓, 2, Enter, ↓, NPV, 8, Enter, ↓, CPT.

The NPV is $9,827.21.

35.   D is the answer, by definition (consecutive payments of the same amount flowing in the same direction).

36.   C is the answer.

On the HP-12C, press 10000, blue g, CFo, 6000, blue g, CFj, 9, blue g, Nj, 7, i, yellow f, NPV.

On the HP-10B II, press 10000, CF_j, 6000, CF_j, 9, shift, N_j, 7, I/YR, shift, NPV.

On the HP-17B II, with the #T? function on, press 10000, INPUT, 6000, INPUT, 9, INPUT, EXIT, the CALC menu key, 7, the I% menu key, the NPV menu key.

On the BA-II Plus, press CF, 10000, Enter, ↓, 6000, Enter, ↓, 9, Enter, ↓, NPV, 7, Enter, ↓, CPT.

The NPV is $49,091.39.

37.   A is the answer. First calculate the inflation-adjusted interest rate (1.08 ÷ 1.05 - 1 x 100) and enter it as the interest rate for the problem. Also, enter 10 as the value of n or N. Enter $20,000 as the beginning-of-period PMT and solve for PV, which is $176,765. Since this is an end-of-period problem, divide this answer by 1.08 to produce the answer, $163,671.08.

38.   D is the answer. First, calculate the adjusted discount rate and enter it into the calculator as the interest rate (including the minus sign).

$$1.06 \div 1.10 - 1 \times 100 = -3.6364$$

Then enter 6 as the value of n or N and 2000 as the beginning-of-year PMT. Compute the PV, which is $13,191. Enter 6 as the interest rate. Also, press 0 and PMT. Compute FV, which is $18,711.

39.   B is the answer, by definition. The net present value is found by subtracting the present value of the outflows from the present value of the inflows associated with the investment.

40.   A is the answer.

On the HP-12C, press 20000, CHS, blue g, CFo, 5000, CHS, blue g, CFj, 1000, blue g, CFj, 12000, blue g, CFj, 30000, blue g, CFj, 9, i, yellow f, NPV.

On the HP-10B II, press 20000, +/-, CF_j, 5000, +/-, CF_j, 1000, CF_j, 12000, CF_j, 30000, CF_j, 9, I/YR, shift, NPV.

On the HP-17B II, with the #T? function on, press 20000, +/-, INPUT, 5000, +/-, INPUT, 1, INPUT, 1000, INPUT, 1 INPUT, 12000, INPUT, 1, INPUT, 30000, INPUT, 1, INPUT, EXIT, the CALC menu key, 9, the I% menu key, the NPV menu key.

On the BA-II Plus, press CF, 20000, +/-, Enter, ↓, 5000, +/-, Enter, ↓, ↓, 1000, Enter, ↓, ↓, 12000, Enter, ↓, ↓, 30000, Enter, ↓, ↓, NPV, 9, Enter, ↓, CPT.

NPV = $6,773.48.

41.   A is the answer. All three statements correctly describe the internal rate of return.

42.   E is the answer. Generally the NPV is the more reliable technique, so (2) is incorrect. The IRR technique does not require a discount rate to perform the calculation, so (3) is incorrect.

43.   A is the answer. All of these considerations should be included in the analysis.

44.   B is the answer. The first project *probably* should be rejected because the discount rate being used is insufficient to reflect the high level of risk of the project. The second project definitely should not be accepted because it is expected to reduce the wealth of the investor in terms of the time value of money.

45.   C is the answer. The present value of the outflows is $20,000 plus $3,000 for 2 years at 7%, or $22,620.32. The terminal or future value of the inflows is $35,000 plus $5,000 for 2 years at 7%, or $40,724.50. With 3 as the value of n or N, the interest rate, the MIRR, is 21.65%.

46.   B is the answer. Each compounding period's interest earnings are added to and become part of the principal for purposes of future interest earnings.

47.   C is the answer. (2) is incorrect because with monthly compounding, a greater total amount of interest is charged per year than with quarterly compounding. Stated differently, the effective interest rate is higher with monthly compounding.

48.   C is the answer. If compounding occurs more than once per year, the effective rate is higher than the nominal rate, so A, B, D, and E are incorrect.

49.   C is the answer. Based on the formula for computing the effective rate, the calculation would be as follows:

$$\text{Effective rate} = \left[1 + \frac{.06}{12}\right]^{12} - 1$$

$$= (1.005)^{12} - 1$$

$$= 1.0617 - 1$$

$$= .0617, \text{ or } 6.17\%$$

On a financial calculator, use the procedure described in paras. 150-155 of the chapter. The rate, with four decimal places displayed, is 6.1678%.

50.   D is the answer. (2) and (3) are incorrect because present values become smaller as discounting frequency and the effective interest rate increase.

51.   D is the answer. Because of quarterly compounding, i is divided by 4, and n is multiplied by 4 in the usual FVSS formula.

52.   C is the answer. Dividing i by 4 gives 3%, and multiplying n by 4 gives 32 periods.

53.   B is the answer. A is incorrect because the cash flows are not level and because compounding frequency is not monthly, as is the cash flow frequency. C is incorrect because the cash flows constitute a simple annuity, not a simple annuity due. D is incorrect because the cash flows constitute a complex annuity due, not a simple annuity due.

APPENDIX A

KEYSTROKES FOR SOLVING SELECTED TVM PROBLEMS USING THE HP-12C CALCULATOR

Note: The individual keystrokes listed in this appendix are separated by commas.

1. Preliminary "housekeeping" and miscellaneous chores

   a. Clearing memory
      yellow f, REG or yellow f, FIN

   b. Setting number of decimal places
      yellow f, desired number

   c. Clearing display or eliminating last entry
      CLX

   d. Raising a number to a power
      base number, ENTER, exponent, y^x

2. Future value of a single sum problems

   a. Finding FVSS
      amount of present value, CHS, PV, number of periods, n, periodic interest rate, i, FV

   b. Finding approximate n (number of periods)
      amount of present value, CHS, PV, amount of future value, FV, periodic interest rate, i, n

   c. Finding i (periodic interest rate)
      amount of present value, CHS, PV, amount of future value, FV, number of periods, n, i

3.   Present value of a single sum problems

    a.   Finding PVSS
        amount of future value, FV, number of
        periods, n, periodic interest rate, i, PV

    b.   Finding approximate n (number of periods)
        see 2.b. above

    c.   Finding i (periodic interest rate)
        see 2.c. above

4.   Future value of an annuity problems

    a.   Finding FVA
        amount of one payment, CHS, PMT,
        periodic interest rate, i, number of
        payments, n, blue g, END, FV

    b.   Finding approximate n (number of payments)
        future value of the annuity, FV, amount
        of one payment, CHS, PMT, blue g,
        END, periodic interest rate, i, n

    c.   Finding i (periodic interest rate)
        future value of the annuity, FV, amount
        of one payment, CHS, PMT, number of
        payments, n, blue g, END, i

5.   Future value of an annuity due problems

    a.   Finding FVAD
        amount of one payment, CHS, PMT,
        periodic interest rate, i, number of
        payments, n, blue g, BEG, FV

    b.   Finding approximate n (number of payments)
        future value of the annuity due, FV,
        amount of one payment, CHS, PMT,
        blue g, BEG, periodic interest rate, i, n

    c.   Finding i (periodic interest rate)
> future value of the annuity due, FV, amount of one payment, CHS, PMT, number of payments, n, blue g, BEG, i

6.   Sinking fund problems

    a.   Finding sinking fund payment
> target amount of sinking fund, FV, periodic interest rate, i, number of payments, n, blue g, BEG (or END), PMT

    b.   Finding approximate n (number of payments)
> target amount of sinking fund, FV, periodic interest rate, i, amount of one payment, CHS, PMT, blue g, BEG (or END), n

    c.   Finding i (periodic interest rate)
> target amount of sinking fund, FV, amount of one payment, CHS, PMT, number of payments, n, blue g, BEG (or END), i

7.   Present value of an annuity problems

    a.   Finding PVA
> amount of one payment, CHS, PMT, periodic interest rate, i, number of payments, n, blue g, END, PV

    b.   Finding approximate n (number of payments)
> present value of the annuity, CHS, PV, amount of one payment, PMT, blue g, END, periodic interest rate, i, n

    c.   Finding i (periodic interest rate)
> present value of the annuity, CHS, PV, amount of one payment, PMT, number of payments, n, blue g, END, i

8. Present value of an annuity due problems

    a. Finding PVAD
        amount of one payment, CHS, PMT, periodic interest rate, i, number of payments, n, blue g, BEG, PV

    b. Finding approximate n (number of payments)
        present value of the annuity due, CHS, PV, amount of one payment, PMT, blue g, BEG, periodic interest rate, i, n

    c. Finding i (periodic interest rate)
        present value of the annuity due, CHS, PV, amount of one payment, PMT, number of payments, n, blue g, BEG, i

9. Debt service/capital sum liquidation problems

    a. Finding the payment
        beginning amount of loan or capital sum, CHS, PV, periodic interest rate, i, number of payments, n, blue g, BEG (or END), PMT

    b. Finding the approximate n (number of payments)
        beginning amount of loan or capital sum, CHS, PV, periodic interest rate, i, amount of one payment, PMT, blue g, BEG (or END), n

    c. Finding i (periodic interest rate)
        beginning amount of loan or capital sum, CHS, PV, amount of one payment, PMT, number of payments, n, blue g, BEG (or END), i

    d. Creating an annual (or monthly) amortization schedule
        annual (or monthly) interest rate, i, original loan amount, CHS, PV, amount of one payment, PMT, blue g, END, 1, yellow f, AMORT (to show the amount

of interest in the first year or month), $x \geq y$ (to show the amount of principal in the first year or month), RCL, PV (to show the unpaid balance of the loan at the end of the first year or month); repeat 1, yellow f, AMORT, $x \geq z$, and RCL, PV to show the interest and principal paid in each succeeding year or month and the unpaid balance of the loan at the end of each year or month

10.   Present value of uneven cash flows problems

a.   Cash flows at end of year
amount of first cash flow, blue g, CFj, number of times it occurs, blue g, Nj, second cash flow, blue g, CFj, number of times it occurs, blue g, Nj, etc. through entire sequence; then interest rate, i, yellow f, NPV

b.   Cash flows at beginning of year
amount of first cash flow, blue g, CFo, number of times it occurs, blue g, Nj, second cash flow, blue g, CFj, number of times it occurs, blue g, Nj, third cash flow, blue g, CFj, number of times it occurs, blue g, Nj, etc. through entire sequence; then interest rate, i, yellow f, NPV

c.   Cash flows that grow by a constant percentage, with first payment made immediately
blue g, BEG, amount of first cash flow, PMT, 1 plus interest rate, ENTER, 1 plus growth rate, ÷, 1, –, 100, x, i, number of payments, n, PV

d.   Cash flows that grow by a constant percentage, with first payment made after one period
divide answer found in 10 c. by (1 plus interest rate)

11.   Future value of uneven cash flows problems

      a.   Generally
                  Compute present value as in 10.a. or b. above; then ENTER, CHS, PV, interest rate, i, number of years, n, FV

      b.   Special case: deposits growing by a constant percentage
                  Compute present value as in 10.c. or d. above; then interest rate, i, 0, PMT, FV

12.   Net present value problems (**Editor's Note**: Each cash flow should be entered as a positive or negative amount, as appropriate.)

      a.   Ungrouped data
                  amount of initial outflow, CHS, blue g, CFo; then amount of each succeeding inflow or outflow, including zeros, pressing blue g and CFj after each (CHS, blue g, and CFj for outflows); then interest rate, i, yellow f, NPV

      b.   Grouped data
                  amount of initial outflow, CHS, blue g, CFo; then amount of first inflow or outflow, including zeros, blue g, CFj (CHS, blue g, CFj for outflows); then number of times that amount occurs in succession, blue g, Nj; repeat the process for each subsequent inflow, outflow, or zero flow or group of same; then interest rate, i, yellow f, NPV

13.   Internal rate of return problems

Same as NPV except for last four keystrokes; instead of (or in addition to) interest rate, i, yellow f, NPV, press yellow f, IRR

14.   Conversion of nominal interest rate to effective interest rate problems

a.   Discrete compounding or discounting
nominal interest rate, ENTER, number of compounding periods per year, n, ÷, i, 100, CHS, ENTER, PV, FV, +

b.   Continuous compounding or discounting during 360-day year
1, ENTER, nominal interest rate, %, blue g, e^x, Δ%

APPENDIX B

KEYSTROKES FOR SOLVING SELECTED TVM PROBLEMS USING THE HP-10B II CALCULATOR

Note: The individual key strokes listed in this appendix are separated by commas.

1.   Preliminary "housekeeping" and miscellaneous chores

    a.   Turning the machine on or off
        ON or shift, OFF

    b.   Clearing a problem or data from memory
        Shift, C ALL

    c.   Setting number of decimal places to be displayed
        Shift, DISP, desired number

    d.   Clearing display screen of an incorrect or unwanted number or error message
        C

    e.   Eliminating last keystroke before entering
        ←

    f.   Setting number of payment periods/ compounding periods per year to one if both are the same
        1, shift, P/YR, C; to check current setting, press shift, C

    g.   Setting the calculator for payments at beginning of period or end of period
        shift, BEG/END; screen will display BEGIN or nothing; to change setting, press shift, BEG/END again

    h.   Raising a number to a power
        base number, shift, y^x, exponent, =

2. Future value of a single sum problems

    a. Finding FVSS
        amount of present value, +/-, PV, number of periods, N, periodic interest rate, I/YR, FV

    b. Finding N (number of periods)
        amount of present value, +/-, PV, amount of future value, FV, periodic interest rate, I/YR, N

    c. Finding I/YR (periodic interest rate)
        amount of present value, +/-, PV, amount of future value, FV, number of periods, N, I/YR

3. Present value of a single sum problems

    a. Finding PVSS
        amount of future value, FV, number of periods, N, periodic interest rate, I/YR, PV

    b. Finding N (number of periods)
        see 2.b., above

    c. Finding I/YR (periodic interest rate)
        see 2.c., above

4. Future value of an annuity problems

    a. Finding FVA
        set the calculator for end-of-period payments (see 1.g., above); set the calculator for one payment/compounding period per year if both are the same (see 1.f., above); amount of one payment, +/-, PMT, periodic interest rate, I/YR, number of payments, N, FV

b.   Finding N (number of payments)
     set the calculator for end-of-period payments (see 1.g., above); set the calculator for one payment/compounding period per year if both are the same (see 1.f., above); amount of one payment, +/-, PMT, periodic interest rate, I/YR, amount of future value, FV, N

c.   Finding I/YR (periodic interest rate)
     set the calculator for end-of-period payments (see 1.g., above); set the calculator for one payment/compounding period per year if both are the same (see 1.f., above); amount of one payment, +/-, PMT, number of payments, N, amount of future value, FV, I/YR

5.   Future value of an annuity due problems

a.   Finding FVAD
     set the calculator for beginning-of-period payments (see 1.g., above); set the calculator for one payment/compounding period per year if both are the same (see 1.f., above); amount of one payment, +/-, PMT, periodic interest rate, I/YR, number of payments, N, FV

b.   Finding N (number of payments)
     set the calculator for beginning-of-period payments (see 1.g., above); set the calculator for one payment/compounding period per year if both are the same (see 1.f., above); amount of one payment, +/-, PMT, periodic interest rate, I/YR, amount of future value, FV, N

c.   Finding I/YR (periodic interest rate)
     set the calculator for beginning-of-period payments (see 1.g., above); set the calculator for one payment/compounding period per year if both are

the same (see 1.f., above); amount of one payment, +/-, PMT, number of payments, N, amount of future value, FV, I/YR

6. Sinking fund problems

    a. Finding sinking fund payment
        set the calculator for beginning-of-period or end-of-period payments, as appropriate (see 1.g., above); set the calculator for one payment/compounding period per year if both are the same (see 1.f., above); target amount of sinking fund, FV, periodic interest rate, I/YR, number of payments, N, PMT

    b. Finding N (number of payments)
        set the calculator for beginning-of-period or end-of-period payments, as appropriate (see 1.g., above); set the calculator for one payment/compounding period per year if both are the same (see 1.f., above); target amount of sinking fund, FV, periodic interest rate, I/YR, amount of one payment, +/-, PMT, N

    c. Finding I/YR (periodic interest rate)
        set the calculator for beginning-of-period or end-of-period payments, as appropriate (see 1.g., above); set the calculator for one payment/compounding period per year if both are the same (see 1.f., above); target amount of sinking fund, FV, number of payments, N, amount of one payment, +/-, PMT, I/YR

7. Present value of an annuity problems

    a. Finding PVA
        set the calculator for end-of-period payments (see 1.g., above); set the calculator for one payment/compounding period per year if both are the same (see

1.f., above); amount of one payment, PMT, periodic interest rate, I/YR, number of payments, N, PV

    b.   Finding N (number of payments)

set the calculator for end-of-period payments (see 1.g., above); set the calculator for one payment/compounding period per year if both are the same (see 1.f., above); amount of one payment, PMT, periodic interest rate, I/YR, amount of present value, +/-, PV, N

    c.   Finding I/YR (periodic interest rate)

set the calculator for end-of-period payments (see 1.g., above); set the calculator for one payment/compounding period per year if both are the same (see 1.f., above); amount of one payment, PMT, number of payments, N, amount of present value, +/-, PV, I/YR

8.   Present value of an annuity due problems

    a.   Finding PVAD

set the calculator for beginning-of-period payments (see 1.g., above); set the calculator for one payment/compounding period per year if both are the same (see 1.f., above); amount of one payment, PMT, periodic interest rate, I/YR, number of payments, N, PV

    b.   Finding N (number of payments)

set the calculator for beginning-of-period payments (see 1.g., above); set the calculator for one payment/compounding period per year if both are the same (see 1.f., above); amount of one payment, PMT, periodic interest rate, I/YR, amount of present value, +/-, PV, N

    c.   Finding I/YR (periodic interest rate)

set the calculator for beginning-of-period payments (see 1.g., above); set the calculator for one payment/compounding period per year if both are the same (see 1.f., above); amount of one payment, PMT, number of payments, N, amount of present value, +/-, PV, I/YR

9. Debt service/capital sum liquidation problems

a. Finding the payment
set the calculator for beginning-of-period or end-of-period payments, as appropriate (see 1.g., above); set the calculator for one payment/compounding period per year if both are the same (see 1.f., above); beginning amount of loan or capital sum, +/-, PV, periodic interest rate, I/YR, number of payments, N, PMT

b. Finding N (number of payments)
set the calculator for beginning-of-period or end-of-period payments, as appropriate (see 1.g., above); set the calculator for one payment/compounding period per year if both are the same (see 1.f., above); beginning amount of loan or capital sum, +/-, PV, periodic interest rate, I/YR, amount of one payment, PMT, N

c. Finding I/YR (periodic interest rate)
set the calculator for beginning-of-period or end-of-period payments, as appropriate (see 1.g., above); set the calculator for one payment/compounding period per year if both are the same (see 1.f., above); beginning amount of loan or capital sum, +/-, PV, number of payments, N, amount of one payment, PMT, I/YR

d.   Creating an amortization schedule
set the calculator for end-of-period payments, (see 1.g., above); set the calculator for one payment/compounding period per year if both are the same (see 1.f., above); number of payments, N, periodic interest rate, I/YR, original amount of the loan, PV, amount of one payment, +/-, PMT, 1, INPUT, shift, AMORT, = (to see total principal paid during first amortization period), =, (to see the amount of interest in the first amortization period), = (to show the unpaid loan balance at the end of the first amortization period), 2, INPUT, shift, AMORT, = (to show the principal paid in the second amortization period), = (to show the amount of interest in the second amortization period), = (to show the unpaid loan balance at the end of the second amortization period), 3, INPUT, shift, AMORT, =, etc. through the loan's final amortization period.

10.   Present value of uneven cash flow problems

a.   Cash flows at end of year
0, CF_j, amount of first cash flow, CF_j, (number of times it occurs if more than once, shift, N_j,) amount of second cash flow, CF_j, (number of times it occurs if more than once, shift, N_j,) amount of third cash flow, etc. through entire sequence; then interest rate, I/YR, shift, NPV

b.   Cash flows at beginning of year
amount of first cash flow, CF_j, amount of second cash flow, CF_j, (number of times it occurs if more than once, shift, N_j,) amount of third cash flow, etc. through entire sequence; then interest rate, I/YR, shift, NPV

c. Cash flows that grow by a constant percentage, with first payment made immediately
set calculator for beginning-of-period payments; amount of first cash flow, PMT, 1 plus interest rate, ÷, 1 plus growth rate, −, 1, x, 100, =, I/YR, number of payments, N, PV

d. Cash flows that grow by a constant percentage, with first payment made after one period
divide answer found in 10.c. above, by (1 plus interest rate)

11. Future value of uneven cash flow problems

a. Generally:
compute present value as in 10.a. or b. above; then +/-, PV, number of periods, N, FV

b. Special case: deposits growing by a constant percentage
Compute present value as in 10.c. or d. above; then interest rate, I/YR, 0, PMT, FV

12. Net present value problems (**Editor's Note:** Each cash flow should be entered as a positive or negative amount, as appropriate.)

use procedure in 10.a. or b. above, but press +/- key after any cash flows that are outflows

13. Internal rate of return problems

same as NPV except for last four keystrokes; instead of (or in addition to) interest rate, I/YR, shift, NPV, press shift, IRR/YR

14. Conversion of nominal interest rate to effective interest rate problems

a. Discrete compounding or discounting

nominal interest rate, shift, NOM%, number of compounding or discounting times per year, shift, P/YR, shift, EFF%; then 1, shift, P/YR, C to restore setting to one payment/compounding period per year and clear the display

b. Continuous compounding or discounting during 360-day year

nominal interest rate, %, shift, e^x, –, 1, x, 100, =

APPENDIX C

KEYSTROKES FOR SOLVING SELECTED TVM PROBLEMS USING THE HP-17B II CALCULATOR

Note: The individual key strokes in this appendix are separated by commas.

1. Preliminary "housekeeping" and miscellaneous chores

    a. Turning the machine on or off
        CLR or colored shift key, OFF

    b. Adjusting contrast on display screen
        hold down CLR, + or -

    c. Selecting the algebraic system of entry logic
        shift, MODES, ALG menu key, EXIT

    d. Returning to main menu
        shift, MAIN or EXIT one or more times

    e. Clearing a problem or data from memory
        menu key for menu to be cleared of problem or data, shift, CLEAR DATA

    f. Setting number of decimal places to be displayed
        DSP, FIX menu key, desired number, INPUT

    g. Clearing display screen
        CLR

    h. Eliminating last keystroke
        ←

i. Setting number of payment periods/ compounding periods per year to one if both are the same

shift, MAIN, FIN menu key, TVM menu key, OTHER menu key, 1, P/YR menu key, shift, MAIN, CLR

j. Setting the calculator for payments at beginning or end of each period

shift, MAIN, FIN menu key, TVM menu key, OTHER menu key, BEG or END menu key, shift, MAIN

k. Raising a number to a power

base number, shift, y^x, exponent, =

2. Future value of a single sum problems

a. Finding FVSS

shift, MAIN, FIN menu key, TVM menu key, number of periods, N menu key, periodic interest rate, I%YR menu key, amount of present value, +/-, PV menu key, FV menu key

b. Finding N (number of periods)

shift, MAIN, FIN menu key, TVM menu key, periodic interest rate, I%YR menu key, amount of present value, +/-, PV menu key, amount of future value, FV menu key, N menu key

c. Finding I%YR (periodic interest rate)

shift, MAIN, FIN menu key, TVM menu key, number of periods, N menu key, amount of present value, +/-, PV menu key, amount of future value, FV menu key, I%YR menu key

3. Present value of a single sum problems

a. Finding PVSS

shift, MAIN, FIN menu key, TVM menu key, number of periods, N menu key, periodic interest rate, I%YR menu key, amount of future value, FV menu key, PV menu key

b.   Finding N (number of periods)
       see 2.b. above

c.   Finding I%YR (periodic interest rate)
       see 2.c. above

4.   Future value of an annuity problems

a.   Finding FVA
       set the calculator for end-of-period payments (see 1.j. above); set the calculator for one payment/compounding period per year if both are the same (see 1.i. above); shift, MAIN, FIN menu key, TVM menu key, number of payments, N menu key, periodic interest rate, I%YR menu key, amount of one payment, +/-, PMT menu key, FV menu key

b.   Finding N (number of payments)
       set the calculator for end-of-period payments (see 1.j. above); set the calculator for one payment/compounding period per year if both are the same (see 1.i. above); shift, MAIN, FIN menu key, TVM menu key, periodic interest rate, I%YR menu key, amount of one payment, +/-, PMT menu key, future value of the annuity, FV menu key, N menu key

c.   Finding I%YR (periodic interest rate)
       set the calculator for end-of-period payments (see 1.j. above); set the calculator for one payment/compounding period per year if both are the same (see 1.i. above); shift, MAIN, FIN menu key, TVM menu key, number of payments, N menu key, amount of one payment, +/-,

PMT menu key, future value of the annuity, FV menu key, I%YR menu key

5. Future value of an annuity due problems

    a.   Finding FVAD

set the calculator for beginning-of-period payments (see 1.j. above); set the calculator for one payment/compounding period per year if both are the same (see 1.i. above); shift, MAIN, FIN menu key, TVM menu key, number of payments, N menu key, periodic interest rate, I%YR menu key, amount of one payment, +/-, PMT menu key, FV menu key

    b.   Finding N (number of payments)

set the calculator for beginning-of-period payments (see 1.j. above); set the calculator for one payment/compounding period per year if both are the same (see 1.i. above); shift, MAIN, FIN menu key, TVM menu key, periodic interest rate, I%YR menu key, amount of one payment, +/-, PMT menu key, future value of the annuity, FV menu key, N menu key

    c.   Finding I%YR (periodic interest rate)

set the calculator for beginning-of-period payments (see 1.j. above); set the calculator for one payment/compounding period per year if both are the same (see 1.i. above); shift, MAIN, FIN menu key, TVM menu key, number of payments, N menu key, amount of one payment, +/-, PMT menu key, future value of the annuity, FV menu key, I%YR menu key

6. Sinking fund problems

    a.   Finding sinking fund payment

set the calculator for beginning-of-period or end-of-period payments, as appropriate (see 1.j. above); set the calculator for one payment/compounding period per year if both are the same (see 1.i. above); shift, MAIN, FIN menu key, TVM menu key, target amount of sinking fund, FV menu key, periodic interest rate, I%YR menu key, number of payments, N menu key, PMT menu key

b. Finding N (number of payments)

set the calculator for beginning-of-period or end-of-period payments, as appropriate (see 1.j. above); set the calculator for one payment/compounding period per year if both are the same (see 1.i. above); target amount of sinking fund, FV menu key, periodic interest rate, I%YR menu key, amount of one payment, +/-, PMT menu key, N menu key

c. Finding I%YR (periodic interest rate)

set the calculator for beginning-of-period or end-of-period payments, as appropriate (see 1.j. above); set the calculator for one payment/compounding period per year if both are the same (see 1.i. above); target amount of sinking fund, FV menu key, number of payments, N menu key, amount of one payment, +/-, PMT menu key, I%YR menu key

7. Present value of an annuity problems

a. Finding PVA

set the calculator for end-of-period payments (see 1.j. above); set the calculator for one payment/compounding period per year if both are the same (see 1.i. above); shift, MAIN, FIN menu key, TVM menu key, number of payments, N menu key, periodic interest rate, I%YR menu key, amount of one payment, PMT menu key, PV menu key

b.   Finding N (number of payments)

set the calculator for end-of-period payments (see 1.j. above); set the calculator for one payment/compounding period per year if both are the same (see 1.i. above); shift, MAIN, FIN menu key, TVM menu key, periodic interest rate, I%YR menu key, present value of the annuity, +/-, PV menu key, amount of one payment, PMT menu key, N menu key

c.   Finding I%YR (periodic interest rate)

set the calculator for end-of-period payments (see 1.j. above); set the calculator for one payment/compounding period per year if both are the same (see 1.i. above); shift, MAIN, FIN menu key, TVM menu key, number of payments, N menu key, present value of the annuity, +/-, PV menu key, amount of one payment, PMT menu key, I%YR menu key

8.   Present value of an annuity due problems

a.   Finding PVAD

set the calculator for beginning-of-period payments (see 1.j. above); set the calculator for one payment/compounding period per year if both are the same (see 1.i. above); shift, MAIN, FIN menu key, TVM menu key, number of payments, N menu key, periodic interest rate, I%YR menu key, amount of one payment, PMT menu key, PV menu key

b.   Finding N (number of payments)

set the calculator for beginning-of-period payments (see 1.j. above); set the calculator for one payment/compounding period per year if both are the same (see 1.i. above); shift, MAIN, FIN menu key, TVM menu key, periodic interest rate, I%YR menu key, amount of one payment, PMT menu key, present value of the annuity, +/-, PV menu key, N menu key

c.   Finding I%YR (periodic interest rate)

set the calculator for beginning-of-period payments (see 1.j. above); set the calculator for one payment/compounding period per year if both are the same (see 1.i. above); shift, MAIN, FIN menu key, TVM menu key, number of payments, N menu key, amount of one payment, PMT menu key, present value of the annuity, +/-, PV menu key, I%YR menu key

9.   Debt service/capital sum liquidation problems

a.   Finding the payment

set the calculator for beginning-of-period or end-of-period payments, as appropriate (see 1.j. above); set the calculator for one payment/compounding period per year if both are the same (see 1.i above); shift, MAIN, FIN menu key, TVM menu key, beginning amount of loan or capital sum, +/-, PV menu key, periodic interest rate, I%YR menu key, number of payments, N menu key, PMT menu key

b.   Finding N (number of payments)

set the calculator for beginning-of-period or end-of-period payments, as appropriate (see 1.j. above); set the calculator for one payment/compounding period per year if both are the same (see 1.i above); shift, MAIN, FIN menu key, TVM menu key, beginning amount of loan or capital sum, +/-, PV menu key, periodic interest rate, I%YR menu key, amount of one payment, PMT menu key, N menu key

c.   Finding I%YR (periodic interest rate)

set the calculator for beginning-of-period or end-of-period payments, as appropriate (see 1.j. above); set the calculator for one payment/compounding period per year if both are the same (see 1.i above); shift, MAIN, FIN menu key, TVM menu key, beginning amount of loan or capital sum, +/-, PV menu key, amount of one payment, PMT menu key, number of payments, N menu key, I%YR menu key

d.   Creating a loan amortization schedule

set the calculator for end-of-period payments (see 1.j. above); set the calculator for one payment/compounding period per year if both are the same (see 1.i. above); FIN menu key, TVM menu key, total number of payments, N menu key, periodic interest rate, I%YR menu key, original loan amount, +/-, PV menu key, amount of one payment, PMT menu key, OTHER menu key, AMRT menu key, 1, #P menu key, INT menu key to see total interest paid during first amortization period, PRIN menu key to show total principal repaid during first amortization period, BAL menu key to show unpaid balance at end of first amortization period, NEXT menu key to perform calculations applicable to next amortization period, INT menu key to see total interest paid during second amortization period, PRIN menu key to see total principal paid during second amortization period, BAL menu key to show unpaid balance at end of second amortization period, NEXT, etc. to end of loan period

10.   Present value of uneven cash flows problems

    a.   Cash flows at end of year

shift, MAIN, FIN menu key, CFLO menu key, #T? menu key to ON, shift, CLEAR DATA, YES menu key, 0, INPUT, amount of first cash flow, INPUT, number of times it occurs, INPUT, amount of second cash flow, INPUT, number of times it occurs, INPUT, amount of third cash flow, INPUT, number of times it occurs, INPUT, etc. through entire sequence; then EXIT, CALC menu key, periodic interest rate, I% menu key, NPV menu key

    b.   Cash flows at beginning of year

shift, MAIN, FIN menu key, CFLO menu key, #T? menu key to ON, shift, CLEAR DATA, YES menu key, amount of first cash flow, INPUT, amount of second cash flow (or amount of first cash flow if it is grouped data), INPUT, number of times it occurs (minus 1 if it is a continuation of the grouped data in the first cash flow), INPUT, amount of next cash flow, INPUT, number of times it occurs, INPUT, etc. through the entire sequence; then EXIT, CALC menu key, periodic interest rate, I% menu key, NPV menu key

    c.   Cash flows that grow by a constant percentage, with first payment made immediately

set the calculator for beginning-of-period payments (see 1.j. above); set the calculator for one payment/compounding period per year if both are the same (see 1.i. above); shift, MAIN, FIN menu key, TVM menu key, amount of first cash flow, PMT menu key, 1 plus periodic interest rate, ÷, 1 plus growth rate, −, 1, x, 100, =, I%YR menu key, number of payments, N menu key, PV menu key

d. Cash flows that grow by a constant percentage, with first payment made after one period

divide answer found in 10.c. by (1 plus periodic interest rate)

11. Future value of uneven cash flows problems

a. Cash flows at end of year

use procedure in 10.a., except for the final keystroke, which should be the NFV menu key, rather than the NPV menu key

b. Cash flows at beginning of year

multiply answer found in 11.a. by (1 plus periodic interest rate)

c. Deposits growing by a constant percentage

compute present value as in 10.c. or d. above; then periodic interest rate, I%YR menu key, 0, PMT menu key, FV menu key

12. Net present value problems (**Editor's Note:** Each cash flow should be entered as a positive or negative amount, as appropriate.)

use procedure in 10.a. or b. above, but press +/- key after any cash flows that are outflows

13. Internal rate of return problems

same as NPV except for last 3 keystrokes; instead of (or in addition to) periodic interest rate, I% menu key, and NPV menu key, press IRR menu key

14. Conversion of nominal interest rate to effective interest rate problems

> shift, MAIN, ICNV menu key, PER or CONT menu key, depending on whether compounding is periodic or continuous, nominal interest rate, NOM% menu key, number of compounding periods per year, P menu key, EFF% menu key

APPENDIX D

KEYSTROKES FOR SOLVING SELECTED TVM PROBLEMS USING THE BA-II PLUS CALCULATOR

Note: The individual keystrokes in this appendix are separated by commas.

1. Preliminary "housekeeping" and miscellaneous chores

    a. Clearing memory
        2nd, MEM, 2nd, CLR Work

    b. Entering and clearing the standard-calculator mode
        2nd, QUIT, 2nd, CLR TVM

    c. Entering and clearing the prompted-worksheet mode
        CF, 2nd, CLR Work (to compute NPV or IRR in uneven cash flow problems)

        OR

        2nd, Amort, 2nd, CLR Work (to solve amortization problems)

    d. Setting number of decimal places to be displayed
        2nd, Format, desired number of decimal places, ENTER

    e. Clearing display of an incorrect or unwanted number or an error message
        CE/C (one or more times)

    f. Eliminating last keystroke before entering
        →

    g. Clearing a problem or data from memory

(1) Clearing a problem or data while in the standard-calculator mode

2nd, CLR TVM, CE/C

(2) Clearing a problem or data while in the prompted-worksheet mode

CF, 2nd, CLR Work

OR

2nd, Amort, 2nd, CLR Work

h. Setting number of payment periods/ compounding periods per year to one if both are the same

2nd, P/Y, 1, ENTER, ↓, 1, ENTER

i. Setting the calculator for payments at beginning of period or end of period

2nd, BGN; if current setting is acceptable, 2nd, QUIT; if not, 2nd, SET, 2nd, QUIT

j. Raising a number to a power

base number, y^x, exponent, =

2. Future value of a single sum problems

a. Finding FVSS

amount of present value, +/-, PV, number of periods, N, periodic interest rate, I/Y, CPT, FV

b. Finding N (number of periods)

amount of present value, +/-, PV, amount of future value, FV, periodic interest rate, I/Y, CPT, N

c. Finding I/Y (periodic interest rate)

amount of present value, +/-, PV, amount of future value, FV, number of periods, N, CPT, I/Y

3.   Present value of a single sum problems

   a.   Finding PVSS
              amount of future value, FV, number of periods, N, periodic interest rate, I/Y, CPT, PV

   b.   Finding N (number of periods)
              see 2.b. above

   c.   Finding I/Y (periodic interest rate)
              see 2.c. above

4.   Future value of an annuity problems

   a.   Finding FVA
              set the calculator for end-of-period payments (see 1.i. above); set the calculator for one payment/compounding period per year if both are the same (see 1.h. above); amount of one payment, +/-, PMT, periodic interest rate, I/Y, number of payments, N, CPT, FV

   b.   Finding N (number of payments)
              set the calculator for end-of-period payments (see 1.i. above); set the calculator for one payment/compounding period per year if both are the same (see 1.h. above); future value of the annuity, FV, amount of one payment, +/-, PMT, periodic interest rate, I/Y, CPT, N

   c.   Finding I/Y (periodic interest rate)
              set the calculator for end-of-period payments (see 1.i. above); set the calculator for one payment/compounding period per year if both are the same (see 1.h. above); future value of the annuity, FV, amount of one payment, +/-, PMT, number of payments, N, CPT, I/Y

5.   Future value of an annuity due problems

    a.   Finding FVAD
set the calculator for beginning-of-period payments (see 1.i. above); set the calculator for one payment/compounding period per year if both are the same (see 1.h. above); amount of one payment, +/-, PMT, periodic interest rate, I/Y, number of payments, N, CPT, FV

    b.   Finding N (number of payments)
set the calculator for beginning-of-period payments (see 1.i. above); set the calculator for one payment/compounding period per year if both are the same (see 1.h. above); future value of the annuity due, FV, amount of one payment, +/-, PMT, periodic interest rate, I/Y, CPT, N

    c.   Finding I/Y (periodic interest rate)
set the calculator for beginning-of-period payments (see 1.i. above); set the calculator for one payment/compounding period per year if both are the same (see 1.h. above); future value of the annuity due, FV, amount of one payment, +/-, PMT, number of payments, N, CPT, I/Y

6.   Sinking fund problems

    a.   Finding sinking fund payment
set the calculator for beginning-of-period payments or end-of-period payments, as appropriate (see 1.i. above); set the calculator for one payment/compounding period per year if both are the same (see 1.h. above); target amount of sinking fund, FV, periodic interest rate, I/Y, number of payments, N, CPT, PMT

b.   Finding N (number of payments)

set the calculator for beginning-of-period payments or end-of-period payments, as appropriate (see 1.i. above); set the calculator for one payment/compounding period per year if both are the same (see 1.h. above); target amount of sinking fund, FV,- periodic interest rate, I/Y, amount of one payment, +/-, PMT, CPT, N

c.   Finding I/Y (periodic interest rate)

set the calculator for beginning-of-period payments or end-of-period payments, as appropriate (see 1.i. above); set the calculator for one payment/compounding period per year if both are the same (see 1.h. above); target amount of sinking fund, FV, amount of one payment, +/-, PMT, number of payments, N, CPT, I/Y

7.   Present value of an annuity problems

a.   Finding PVA

set the calculator for end-of-period payments (see 1.i. above); set the calculator for one payment/compounding period per year if both are the same (see 1.h. above); amount of one payment, +/-, PMT, periodic interest rate, I/Y, number of payments, N, CPT, PV

b.   Finding N (number of payments)

set the calculator for end-of-period payments (see 1.i. above); set the calculator for one payment/compounding period per year if both are the same (see 1.h. above); present value of the annuity, +/-, PV, amount of one payment, PMT, periodic interest rate, I/Y, CPT, N

c.   Finding I/Y (periodic interest rate)
set the calculator for end-of-period payments (see 1.i. above); set the calculator for one payment/compounding period per year if both are the same (see 1.h. above); present value of the annuity, +/-, PV, amount of one payment, PMT, number of payments, N, CPT, I/Y

8.   Present value of an annuity due problems

a.   Finding PVAD
set the calculator for beginning-of-period payments (see 1.i. above); set the calculator for one payment/compounding period per year if both are the same (see 1.h. above); amount of one payment, +/-, PMT, periodic interest rate, I/Y, number of payments, N, CPT, PV

b.   Finding N (number of payments)
set the calculator for beginning-of-period payments (see 1.i. above); set the calculator for one payment/compounding period per year if both are the same (see 1.h. above); present value of the annuity, +/-, PV, amount of one payment, PMT, periodic interest rate, I/Y, CPT, N

c.   Finding I/Y (periodic interest rate)
set the calculator for beginning-of-period payments (see 1.i. above); set the calculator for one payment/compounding period per year if both are the same (see 1.h. above); present value of the annuity, +/-, PV, amount of one payment, PMT, number of payments, N, CPT, I/Y

9.   Debt service/capital sum liquidation problems

   a.   Finding the payment
         set the calculator for beginning-of-period payments or end-of-period payments, as appropriate (see 1.i. above); set the calculator for one payment/compounding period per year if both are the same (see 1.h. above); beginning amount of loan or capital sum, +/-, PV, periodic interest rate, I/Y, number of payments, N, CPT, PMT

   b.   Finding N (number of payments)
         set the calculator for beginning-of period payments or end-of-period payments, as appropriate (see 1.i. above); set the calculator for one payment/compounding period per year if both are the same (see 1.h. above); beginning amount of loan or capital sum, +/-, PV, periodic interest rate, I/Y, amount of one payment, PMT, CPT, N

   c.   Finding I/Y (periodic interest rate)
         set the calculator for beginning-of-period payments or end-of-period payments, as appropriate (see 1.i. above); set the calculator for one payment/compounding period per year if both are the same (see 1.h. above); beginning amount of loan or capital sum, +/-, PV, amount of one payment, PMT, number of payments, N, CPT, I/Y

   d.   Creating an amortization schedule
         set the calculator for end-of-period payments (see 1.i. above); set the calculator for one payment/compounding period per year if both are the same (see 1.h. above); 2nd, QUIT, beginning amount of loan, +/-, PV, periodic interest rate, I/Y, number of payments, N, amount of one payment, PMT, 2nd,

Amort, 2nd, CLR Work, 1, ENTER, ↓, 1, ENTER, ↓, (shows unpaid loan principal after first amortization period), ↓ (shows amount paid on principal in first amortization period), ↓ (shows amount paid as interest in first amortization period), ↓, ↓, 2, ENTER, ↓ (shows unpaid loan principal after second amortization period), ↓ (shows total amount paid on principal during first two amortization periods), ↓ (shows total amount paid as interest during first two amortization periods), ↓, ↓, 3, ENTER, etc. Repeat this process throughout the loan's duration to show the gradually declining loan balance at the end of each amortization period, the total amount applied on principal to that point, and the total amount paid as interest to that point.

10. Present value of uneven cash flows problems

   a. Cash flows at end of period

   CF, 2nd, CLR Work, ENTER, ↓, amount of first cash flow, ENTER, ↓, number of times it occurs, ENTER, ↓, amount of second cash flow, ENTER, ↓, number of times it occurs, ENTER, ↓, amount of third cash flow, ENTER, ↓, number of times it occurs, ENTER, ↓, etc. through entire sequence; then NPV, periodic interest rate, ENTER, ↓, CPT

   b. Cash flows at beginning of period

   CF, 2nd, CLR Work, amount of first cash flow, ENTER, ↓, amount of second cash flow (or amount of first cash flow if it is grouped data), ENTER, ↓, number of times it occurs (minus 1 if it is a continuation of the grouped data in the first cash flow), ENTER, ↓, amount of third cash flow, ENTER, ↓, number of times it occurs, ENTER, ↓, etc.

> through entire sequence; then NPV, periodic interest rate, ENTER, ↓, CPT

    c.   Cash flows that grow by a constant percentage, with first payment made immediately
> set the calculator for beginning-of-period payments (see 1.i. above); set the calculator for one payment/compounding period per year if both are the same (see 1.h. above); amount of first cash flow, PMT, 1 plus periodic interest rate, ÷, 1 plus growth rate, -, 1, x, 100, =, I/Y, number of payments, N, CPT, PV

    d.   Cash flows that grow by a constant percentage, with first payment made after one period
> divide answer found in 10.c. by (1 plus periodic interest rate)

11.   Future value of uneven cash flows problems

    a.   Generally:
> compute present value as in 10.a. or b. above; then STO, 1, CF, 2nd, CLR Work, 2nd, QUIT, RCL, 1, +/-, PV, periodic interest rate, I/Y, number of payments, N, CPT, FV

    b.   Special case: deposits growing by a constant percentage
> compute present value as in 10.c. or d. above; then interest rate, I/Y, 0, PMT, CPT, FV

12.   Net present value problems **(Editor's Note**: Each cash flow should be entered as a positive or negative amount, as appropriate.)
> use procedure in 10.a. or b. above, but press +/- key after any cash flows that are outflows

13.   Internal rate of return problems
> same as NPV except for (or in addition to) last five keystrokes; instead of (or after) pressing

NPV, interest rate, ENTER, ↓, and CPT, press IRR, CPT

14. Conversion of nominal interest rate to effective interest rate problems

    a. Discrete compounding or discounting
2nd, I Conv, 2nd, CLR Work, nominal interest rate, ENTER, ↓, ↓, number of compounding periods per year, ENTER, ↑, CPT

    b. Continuous compounding
nominal interest rate, %, 2nd, e^x, −, 1, x, 100, =

APPENDIX E

TABLE OF EFFECTIVE INTEREST RATES

Table E
Effective Annual Interest Rates

NOMINAL ANNUAL INTEREST RATE	SEMI-ANNUALLY	QUARTERLY	MONTHLY	WEEKLY	DAILY (360)	CONTINUOUS (360)
0.25%	0.25016%	0.25023%	0.25029%	0.25031%	0.25031%	0.25031%
0.50%	0.50063%	0.50094%	0.50118%	0.50123%	0.50128%	0.50128%
0.75%	0.75141%	0.75211%	0.75258%	0.75277%	0.75281%	0.75282%
1.00%	1.00250%	1.00376%	1.00460%	1.00492%	1.00500%	1.00502%
1.25%	1.25391%	1.25587%	1.25719%	1.25769%	1.25782%	1.25785%
1.50%	1.50562%	1.50846%	1.51036%	1.51109%	1.51127%	1.51131%
1.75%	1.75766%	1.76152%	1.76410%	1.76510%	1.76536%	1.76540%
2.00%	2.01000%	2.01505%	2.01844%	2.01974%	2.02008%	2.02013%
2.25%	2.26266%	2.26906%	2.27335%	2.27501%	2.27543%	2.27550%
2.50%	2.51562%	2.52354%	2.52885%	2.53090%	2.53142%	2.53151%
2.75%	2.76891%	2.77849%	2.78493%	2.78741%	2.78805%	2.78816%
3.00%	3.02250%	3.03392%	3.04160%	3.04456%	3.04532%	3.04545%
3.25%	3.27641%	3.28982%	3.29885%	3.30234%	3.30324%	3.30339%
3.50%	3.53063%	3.54621%	3.55670%	3.56076%	3.56179%	3.56197%
3.75%	3.78516%	3.80306%	3.81513%	3.81980%	3.82100%	3.82120%
4.00%	4.04000%	4.06040%	4.07415%	4.07948%	4.08085%	4.08108%
4.25%	4.29516%	4.31822%	4.33377%	4.33979%	4.34134%	4.34161%
4.50%	4.55063%	4.57651%	4.59398%	4.60075%	4.60249%	4.60279%
4.75%	4.80641%	4.83528%	4.85479%	4.86235%	4.86429%	4.86462%
5.00%	5.06250%	5.09453%	5.11619%	5.12458%	5.12674%	5.12711%
5.25%	5.31891%	5.35427%	5.37819%	5.38747%	5.38985%	5.39026%
5.50%	5.57562%	5.61448%	5.64079%	5.65099%	5.65362%	5.65406%
5.75%	5.83266%	5.87518%	5.90398%	5.91516%	5.91804%	5.91853%
6.00%	6.09000%	6.13636%	6.16778%	6.17998%	6.18312%	6.18365%
6.25%	6.34766%	6.39802%	6.43218%	6.44545%	6.44887%	6.44945%
6.50%	6.60562%	6.66016%	6.69719%	6.71157%	6.71528%	6.71590%
6.75%	6.86391%	6.92279%	6.96279%	6.97834%	6.98235%	6.98303%
7.00%	7.12250%	7.18590%	7.22901%	7.24577%	7.25009%	7.25082%

Table E (Cont'd)
Effective Annual Interest Rates

NOMINAL ANNUAL INTEREST RATE	COMPOUNDING FREQUENCY					
	SEMI-ANNUALLY	QUAR-TERLY	MONTHLY	WEEKLY	DAILY (360)	CONTINUOUS (360)
7.25%	7.38141%	7.44950%	7.49583%	7.51385%	7.51850%	7.51928%
7.50%	7.64063%	7.71359%	7.76326%	7.78259%	7.78757%	7.78842%
7.75%	7.90016%	7.97816%	8.03130%	8.05199%	8.05732%	8.05822%
8.00%	8.16000%	8.24322%	8.29995%	8.32205%	8.32774%	8.32871%
8.25%	8.42016%	8.50876%	8.56921%	8.59277%	8.59884%	8.59987%
8.50%	8.68062%	8.77480%	8.83909%	8.86415%	8.87061%	8.87171%
8.75%	8.94141%	9.04132%	9.10958%	9.13620%	9.14307%	9.14423%
9.00%	9.20250%	9.30833%	9.38069%	9.40892%	9.41620%	9.41743%
9.25%	9.46391%	9.57583%	9.65241%	9.68230%	9.69001%	9.69131%
9.50%	9.72563%	9.84383%	9.92476%	9.95635%	9.96451%	9.96589%
9.75%	9.98766%	10.11231%	10.19772%	10.23108%	10.23969%	10.24114%
10.00%	10.25000%	10.38129%	10.47131%	10.50648%	10.51556%	10.51709%
10.25%	10.51266%	10.65076%	10.74551%	10.78255%	10.79211%	10.79373%
10.50%	10.77563%	10.92072%	11.02035%	11.05930%	11.06936%	11.07106%
10.75%	11.03891%	11.19118%	11.29580%	11.33673%	11.34730%	11.34909%
11.00%	11.30250%	11.46213%	11.57188%	11.61484%	11.62593%	11.62781%
11.25%	11.56641%	11.73357%	11.84859%	11.89363%	11.90526%	11.90723%
11.50%	11.83063%	12.00551%	12.12593%	12.17310%	12.18528%	12.18734%
11.75%	12.09516%	12.27795%	12.40390%	12.45326%	12.46601%	12.46816%
12.00%	12.36000%	12.55088%	12.68250%	12.73410%	12.74743%	12.74969%
12.25%	12.62516%	12.82431%	12.96174%	13.01563%	13.02956%	13.03191%
12.50%	12.89063%	13.09824%	13.24160%	13.29785%	13.31239%	13.31485%
12.75%	13.15641%	13.37267%	13.52211%	13.58076%	13.59592%	13.59849%
13.00%	13.42250%	13.64759%	13.80328%	13.86436%	13.88017%	13.88284%
13.25%	13.68891%	13.92302%	14.08503%	14.14866%	14.16512%	14.16790%
13.50%	13.95563%	14.19894%	14.36744%	14.43366%	14.45078%	14.45368%
13.75%	14.22266%	14.47537%	14.65050%	14.71935%	14.73716%	14.74017%
14.00%	14.49000%	14.75230%	14.93420%	15.00574%	15.02425%	15.02738%

Table E (Cont'd)
Effective Annual Interest Rates

NOMINAL ANNUAL INTEREST RATE	SEMI-ANNUALLY	QUAR-TERLY	MONTHLY	WEEKLY	DAILY (360)	CONTINUOUS (360)
			COMPOUNDING FREQUENCY			
14.25%	14.75766%	15.02973%	15.21855%	15.29284%	15.31206%	15.31531%
14.50%	15.02563%	15.30766%	15.50354%	15.58063%	15.60058%	15.60396%
14.75%	15.29391%	15.58610%	15.78917%	15.86913%	15.88983%	15.89333%
15.00%	15.56250%	15.86504%	16.07545%	16.15834%	16.17979%	16.18342%
15.25%	15.83141%	16.14449%	16.36238%	16.44825%	16.47049%	16.47425%
15.50%	16.10063%	16.42444%	16.64996%	16.73888%	16.76190%	16.76580%
15.75%	16.37016%	16.70489%	16.93820%	17.03021%	17.05404%	17.05808%
16.00%	16.64000%	16.98586%	17.22708%	17.32226%	17.34692%	17.35109%
16.25%	16.91016%	17.26733%	17.51662%	17.61503%	17.64052%	17.64483%
16.50%	17.18062%	17.54930%	17.80681%	17.90851%	17.93485%	17.93931%
16.75%	17.45141%	17.83179%	18.09766%	18.20271%	18.22992%	18.23453%
17.00%	17.72250%	18.11478%	18.38917%	18.49762%	18.52573%	18.53048%
17.25%	17.99391%	18.39829%	18.68134%	18.79326%	18.82227%	18.82718%
17.50%	18.26562%	18.68230%	18.97417%	19.08963%	19.11956%	19.12462%
17.75%	18.53766%	18.96682%	19.26766%	19.38671%	19.41758%	19.42281%
18.00%	18.81000%	19.25186%	19.56182%	19.68453%	19.71635%	19.72174%
18.25%	19.08266%	19.53741%	19.85664%	19.98307%	20.01887%	20.02141%
18.50%	19.35563%	19.82347%	20.15212%	20.28235%	20.31613%	20.32184%
18.75%	19.62891%	20.11004%	20.44828%	20.58235%	20.61714%	20.62302%
19.00%	19.90250%	20.39713%	20.74510%	20.88309%	20.91890%	20.92496%
19.25%	20.17641%	20.68473%	21.04259%	21.18457%	21.22141%	21.22765%
19.50%	20.45063%	20.97285%	21.34076%	21.48678%	21.52468%	21.53110%
19.75%	20.72516%	21.26148%	21.63960%	21.78973%	21.82871%	21.83531%
20.00%	21.00000%	21.55063%	21.93911%	22.09343%	22.13349%	22.14028%
20.25%	21.27516%	21.84029%	22.23930%	22.39786%	22.43904%	22.44601%
20.50%	21.55063%	22.13047%	22.54016%	22.70304%	22.74534%	22.75251%
20.75%	21.82641%	22.42117%	22.84171%	23.00897%	23.05242%	23.05977%
21.00%	22.10250%	22.71239%	23.14393%	23.31564%	23.36025%	23.36781%

Table E (Concluded)
Effective Annual Interest Rates

NOMINAL ANNUAL INTEREST RATE	SEMI-ANNUALLY	QUAR-TERLY	MONTHLY	WEEKLY	DAILY (360)	CONTINUOUS (360)
21.25%	22.37891%	23.00413%	23.44684%	23.62307%	23.66886%	23.67661%
21.50%	22.65563%	23.29639%	23.75043%	23.93125%	23.97823%	23.98619%
21.75%	22.93266%	23.58917%	24.05470%	24.24017%	24.28838%	24.29654%
22.00%	23.21000%	23.88247%	24.35966%	24.84986%	24.59930%	24.60767%
22.25%	23.48766%	24.17629%	24.66530%	24.86030%	24.91100%	24.91958%
22.50%	23.76562%	24.47063%	24.97164%	25.17180%	25.22347%	25.23227%
22.75%	24.04391%	24.76550%	25.27866%	25.48346%	25.83672%	25.54574%
23.00%	24.32250%	25.06089%	25.58638%	25.79619%	25.85076%	25.86000%
23.25%	24.60141%	25.35680%	25.89479%	26.10967%	26.16558%	26.17504%
23.50%	24.88063%	25.65324%	26.20389%	26.42393%	26.48118%	26.49088%
23.75%	25.16016%	25.95021%	26.51368%	26.73895%	26.79757%	26.80750%
24.00%	25.44000%	26.24770%	26.82418%	27.05474%	27.11475%	27.12491%
24.25%	25.72016%	26.54571%	27.13537%	27.37131%	27.43272%	27.44312%
24.50%	26.00063%	26.84426%	27.44727%	27.68864%	27.75149%	27.76213%
24.75%	26.28141%	27.14333%	27.75986%	28.00676%	28.07104%	28.08194%
25.00%	26.56250%	27.44293%	28.07316%	28.32565%	28.39140%	28.40254%

Notes